Have your favourite magazine delivered to your door -and save money too.

The Countryman

Takes you to the heart of the country

INCORPORATING COUNTRY ORIGINS

Winters long ago
Lichen hunting
A passion for snowdrops
Over the seas to Staffa
The A to Z of British firewood
The lost art of scree running

Save 20%

when you subscribe

See overleaf for details

I n an ever - changing modern world, it's comforting to know you can receive every single issue of *The Countryman* delivered direct to your home, wherever you live in the world. A subscription also makes the perfect gift for friends or family. Subscribe today and you'll **save 20%** on the full subscription rate - **that's 48p an issue.** And our money back guarantee means we'll refund any unmailed copies if you are not completely satisfied. It's so easy to subscribe - simply complete and post the order form below and we'll do the rest!

	Full price	Discount	You save	You pay
UK	£19.20	20%	£3.90	**£15.30**
Europe	£23.30	20%	£4.70	**£18.60**
USA	$50.00	20%	$10.00	**$40.00**
Rest of the World	£34.10	20%	£6.85	**£27.25**

20W

Subscribe now

Simply complete the coupon and post to:
UK: The Countryman Subscriptions, FREEPOST CY1061, Haywards Heath, West Sussex, RH16 3ZA.
Telephone: +44 (0)1444 445555
Fax: +44 (0)1444 445599
Credit Card Hotline Number: +44 (0)1622 778778

USA: The Countryman Subscriptions Dept, 1327 Alita Lane, Escondido CA 92030 USA.
Telephone: 760 747 8327.

For subscription prices please refer to price grid.

Your details:

Mr/Mrs/Miss/Ms: Forename:

Surname:

Address:

Postcode:

Daytime tel. no. (inc. STD code):
(in case we have a query about your order)

Price £/$:

Gift subscription: (Please also fill in Your details)

Mr/Mrs/Miss/Ms: Forename:

Surname:

Address:

Postcode:

Daytime tel. no. (inc. STD code):
(in case we have a query about your order)

Price £/$:

Payment details:

I enclose a cheque/postal international money order made payable to IPC Magazines Ltd, for the total amount of £/$ _____ Or please debit my:

☐ Visa   ☐ Mastercard   ☐ Amex   ☐ Switch (UK only)

Card no: (Switch UK only)

Expiry date:_____ / _____ Card issue no ☐☐ (Switch UK only)

Signature:
(I am over 18)

This offer is open to new subscribers only and closes on 30th April 2000. Please allow up to 6 weeks for the delivery of your first subscription issue. IPC Magazines Ltd., the publishers of The Countryman, may pass your name and address to other reputable companies whose products and services may be of interest to you. Please tick this box if you prefer not to receive such offers ☐.

The Countryman

March 17-April 27 2000   *Vol. 105, No. 2*

CONTENTS

FEATURES

In search of the siskin   13
John Lawton Roberts on a
lifetime's quest for one of
our most elusive birds

Seals at risk   26
Britain plays host to half the
world's population of grey seals,
yet in some quarters they are very
unpopular. Brian Martin reports

Lunching on pollution   28
Michelle Corps on a natural way to
clean up the land

Down among
the dumplings   42
Jerome Betts on the virtues of a
'fair round belly'

Secrets of
The Garden House   45
Stuart Fraser reveals the
history of a little-known
historic garden

A rag-bag
of recipes   56
H.J. Mason on how to make a
pigeon into a grouse

A nest under the waves   60
Leslie Jackman among
the sticklebacks

The calm
before the swarm   62
Mike Silkstone with some amazing
facts – and fancies – about the
world's most useful insect

Railway memories   65
Eric Cresswell unearths a
fascinating document

A lost literary talent   67
David Evans remembers the poet
and essayist James Farrar

A history of
Happy Families   70
John Wilmot on card
games down the years

Treasured collection   74
Michelle Corps explores the biggest
picture library in the world

The elusive siskin. See page 13.

Spinning in Wales. See page 74.

The cycle of life 37
Stefan Buczacki on destruction,
creation and garden design

Country notes 51
Robin Page on Lark Rise Farm

From the archives... 54
From the archives... 78
Wild life and tame 79
Brian Martin with readers' natural
history observations and queries

**Ramblers'
Association news** 83
Jackie Sanders on the
problem of blocked footpaths

**Curiouser and
curiouser** 86
John Vince with more readers'
mysteries and queries

**One countryman
to another** 90
Readers' stories, and memories
of life earlier this century

Country diary 95
Humphrey Phelps on gumboots
and nightmare regulations

Gardeners' questions... 98
Answered by Val Bourne

Bookshelf 104
New titles reviewed

Looking at nature 110
Peter Marren on what
makes good conservation

A forest for the nation 127
Phil Drabble sings the praises of a
remarkable woodland initiative

**POETRY
Greenhouse** 114
Patricia Pogson

Plaid, truis and tartans 112
Ivor Smullen with a brief history of
Scotland's national dress

**Whatever happened
to Poppyland?** 116
Bel Bailey on the fate
of a Norfolk legend

**REGULARS
Comment** 5
Birds before buds 8
Rusticus suggests we go organic
and save our wildlife

**Subscribe to The
Countryman** 11 & 59
– the perfect gift for
yourself or a friend

Letters to the editor 20
Readers have their say

**Digging round
the country** 31
Francis Pryor visits
the Orkney Isles

Country characters 34
Humphrey Phelps remembers Arch
Ayland, the carrier

EDITORIAL

Editor: Tom Quinn **Editorial assistant:** Lynn Sullivan
Sub editor/Layout: Michelle Corps **Natural history editor:** Brian Martin
Classified advertisements: 020 7261 2897 (Fax: 020 7261 6579)
Marketing manager: Imelda Bye
Associate Publisher: Allison Ganley
Publishing Director: Evelyn Webster

Editorial office: The Countryman, IPC Magazines, King's Reach Tower, Stamford Street, London SE1 9LS (Tel: 020 7261 7265/7262. Fax: 020 7261 7273)
Copyright: 2000 by The Countryman. All rights reserved.
Contributions are welcome, preferably with photographs.
You *must* send an SAE.

SUBSCRIBE BY CREDIT CARD ON 01622 778778 OR SEE PAGE 11

Or write to: The Countryman, **FREEPOST, CY1061, Haywards Heath, Sussex RH16 3ZA** . A year's subscription in the UK is £19.20; £23.30 (Europe by airmail and elsewhere in the World by surface) or £34.10 (rest of world by airmail). In the U.S.A. and Canada it costs $50.00. **Subscribers resident in the US** and Canada should contact The Countryman Subscriptions, 2039 Via Alexandra, Escondido, CA 92026, U.S.A.
NB: if you live in Britain and give a subscription to a friend or relative in the USA you should contact our UK subscription office on 01444 445555.

SUBSCRIPTION PROBLEM?

Ring: 01444 445555

WANT TO ADVERTISE?

Contact Claire Pickard on 020 7261 2897 (Fax: 020 7261 6579)
The Countryman, Room 501, King's Reach Tower, Stamford Street, London SE1 9LS.
For inserts call Innovator on 020 7261 7710.

CAN'T FIND A COPY AT YOUR NEWSAGENT?

Ring 020 7261 7704

For back issues and binders ring John Denton Services: 0870 756 0000

Printed by E.T.Heron & Co Ltd, The Bentall Complex, Colchester Road, Heybridge, Maldon, Essex CM8 7NW. **Distributed** by Marketforce (UK) Ltd, 247 Tottenham Court Rd, London W1P ORU (tel 020 7261 5555)
COVER: Grey seal pup by David Kjaer.

Want to reproduce an article or get a copy of a photo in this issue?

Contact Ruth Grocott on 020 7261 5096

Postmaster please send address corrections to The Countryman, 2039 Via Alexandra, Escondido, CA 92026. Periodicals postage paid at Rahway NJ. (tel for enquiries 001 [if from UK] (760) 747 1438) ISSN 0011-0272

Comment

M y brother, who is a devoted reader of *The Countryman*, tells me that he regularly feels the urge to hurl his copy of the magazine out through the nearest window or into the fire. My 'Comment,' it appears, is the problem: 'Sometimes you sound like an intolerant old bigot,' he says, 'but then along comes the next issue and you sound like an exasperatingly woolly minded liberal'.

I was delighted by this because it reminded me that the founder of this magazine thought it should never toe a particular party line. Robertson Scott argued that the editor should say what he thinks according to the merits of a particular issue and regardless of the boundaries between particular political parties.

Of course some subjects seem to unite right and left. The European Community is a case in point. It goes against the grain to say it but – from a trading point of view – I think the EU is probably a good thing, but when EU bureaucrats start telling us how big our apples have to be or how to cut our hedges it is time to tell them to take a running jump. The apples part of the previous sentence is (I hope) a joke, but the hedge bit – incredibly – is true.

In the midst of all their other woes farmers are now going to lose support funding if they fail to keep their hedges to four metres wide or less. Which brings me to wildlife. The RSPB's latest report landed recently on my desk and it makes depressing reading. Most of our best-loved and once common birds are in serious decline. Loss of habitat is the major reason given. And now we are told that our hedges are to be a maximum of four metres wide. This means that those hedges which are currently of maximum benefit to wildlife (ie the big ones) will be reduced still further and our birds will continue to decline. Many ancient Devon banks – often as much as eight metres wide – may also have to be damaged. A MAFF spokesman told me that they are trying to persuade the (unelected) European Commission to be flexible on the hedge issue, but don't hold your breath.

Less depressing

That RSPB report does include some good news – some species of birds of prey are doing rather well it seems – which reminds me that now spring is well and truly here it won't do to continually write about how depressing things are in the countryside. The truth is that, in Britain, you still don't have to travel that far to enjoy a variety and richness of countryside that is the envy of most of the world. We still make a reasonable job in many areas of combining food production with attractive landscapes. Indeed traditional farming and forestry practice have, over the centuries, contributed enormously to the beauty of our landscape: drystone walls are still built and repaired, hedges are still laid here and there, many houses are still thatched, and ancient roadways still wind between villages and hamlets whose basic outlines have remained unchanged for centuries.

On a recent trip to the South West I walked for a day along the lanes near Moretonhampstead on the southern edge of Dartmoor. Here, just 20 miles from Exeter, I found ancient granite farms lost down deep lanes, hedges thick and tall, and fields shadowing Domesday lines. It was a salutary reminder that for all its faults Britain is still a wonderful place in which to live.

Spring in the churchyard at Fairstead, Essex. Amid stories of rural doom and gloom, there is still much to enjoy in the British countryside.

John Tarlton

A dig at the Dome

I know that criticising the Millennium Dome is a bit like attacking a man when he is down, but I can't resist mentioning the day I tried to ring the Dome Press Office. 'I'm afraid the Dome Press office doesn't answer calls,' a mysterious voice on the information number told me. 'Not even calls from the press?' 'Fraid not,' said the voice. Now doesn't that just sum up everything that's wrong with the Dome. A press office that doesn't talk to the press.

Correction

In his review of the biography of the miner-writer B.L. Coombes (January 28 issue) Humphrey Phelps' quotes B.L. Coombes' reaction to the inquest on the death of a miner: 'I realised that neither collier, solicitors or hardly anyone present had the least idea what happens underground.' The word 'collier' should, of course, have been 'coroner'. Our apologies.

Tom Quinn

Rainbow Flowers
DIRECT FROM Guernsey

DE	CARNATIONS (Mixed Colours)		
10	10 Luxury Carnations	SPECIAL OFFER	£9.95
8	18 Luxury Carnations		£14.00
4	24 Luxury Carnations		£16.95

	FRESIAS (Mixed Colours)		
20	20 Posy Freesias	SPECIAL OFFER	£9.95
20	20 Luxury Freesias		£12.95
30	30 Luxury Freesias		£14.95
50	50 Luxury Freesias		£17.95

	MIXED BOUQUETS (Mixed Colours)		
MM	7 Luxury Carnations & 5 Luxury Fresias	SPECIAL OFFER	£9.95
1	10 Luxury Carnations & 15 Luxury Freesias		£14.95
1	15 Luxury Carnations & 25 Luxury Freesias (as pictured)		£18.95

	ORCHIDS			LUXURY SEASONAL BOUQUETS		
RC10	10 Thai Orchids with Foliage	£14.95	MS	Medium	£14.95
RC15	15 Thai Orchids with Foliage	£19.95	LS	Large	£17.95

ur flowers are carefully selected and wrapped in cellophane, packed with fern, your message, flower food and vase life instructions.

We can pack our Fresh Flowers with ribbon and bow for just £1.00 extra. If you require this, please mark X on the order form.

eliveries to **U.K.** are posted Monday to Friday by First Class Mail and usually take 24 to 48 hours from despatch. Please note - We are not able to deliver on Sunday, lowers posted on Friday will arrive on Saturday or Monday. We cannot guarantee your chosen date of arrival with normal postage and flowers may arrive the day before. Guaranteed date orders can be arranged for delivery Tuesday to Friday at an extra cost of £5.00.

elivery destinations of **Europe, USA & Canada** we can only despatch Carnations. SWIFTAIR Express Mail is used for all overseas destinations at an extra cost of £5.00. Deliveries to **Europe** are posted on Friday for delivery on Tuesday/Wednesday, or Monday for delivery on Thursday/Friday. Deliveries to **USA & Canada** are posted on Friday and are expected to arrive from Tuesday to Thursday.

ERING - Telephone your order or fill in your requirement and post or fax the order form, together with your cheque or card details to the address below

ORDER HOTLINE – 08707 440004
24 HOURS A DAY - 7 DAYS A WEEK. FAX - 01481 725718
INBOW FLOWERS, PO BOX 540, ST PETER PORT, GUERNSEY, GY1 6HG

m Required: Code _____ Ribbon & Bow: ☐ Arrival Date: _____

d to: _____

_____ Postcode: _____

ssage: _____

_____

NDER'S Name _____

dress: _____ Postcode: _____

ur Tel No _____ CM

PAYMENT DETAILS
☐ CHEQUE MADE PAYABLE TO RAINBOW FLOWERS ☐ ACCESS, VISA, SWITCH OR SOLO CARD

RD NUMBER
☐☐☐☐ ☐☐☐☐ ☐☐☐☐ ☐☐☐☐

ALID ROM ☐☐ ☐☐ ISSUE NUMBER (SWITCH ONLY) ☐☐

PIRES ND ☐☐ ☐☐ CARDHOLDER'S SIGNATURE

PLEASE SEND COMPLETED FORM TO :
**RAINBOW FLOWERS,
PO BOX 540,
ST PETER PORT
GUERNSEY, GY1 6HG**

FOR MULTIPLE ORDERS PLEASE WRITE A LETTER DETAILING YOUR EXACT REQUIREMENTS.

Birds before buds

Rusticus suggests we go organic and save our birds

L ast month a kind neighbour brought me a dead bird which she found beneath her window and believed my artist son might like to sketch. I could not determine the cause of death with any certainty, but at least I could tell her that the unfortunate bird was a female bullfinch, which was particularly upsetting as the species has always been one of my favourites.

On returning to my desk I opened the post to find – hot off the press – a copy of *The State of the UK's Birds 1999*, and there on the first page was a large photograph of the handsome male bullfinch. The caption brought more bad news: 'Secretive birds of woodland and hedgerow, numbers of bullfinches have fallen sharply, probably as a result of hedgerow loss and degradation.' It is estimated that the UK bullfinch population has fallen by some 40 per cent since the Common Birds Census began in 1970.

Produced by the two non-governmental organisations most closely involved in breeding bird monitoring in the UK, the Royal Society for the Protection of Birds and the British Trust for Ornithology, this new annual bird report is a most welcome and important document, providing both a broad picture of how Britain's birdlife is faring and analysis of how individual species are decreasing or increasing. Sadly, it shows that while there have been many successes in reviving threatened species, largely through well-targeted conservation effort, so far it has proved impossible to reverse the worrying declines of the most common species. Indeed, the list of widespread species that are candidates for red-listing and priority status, such as the lapwing and house sparrow, is lengthening.

Not surprisingly, agriculture is singled out for special criticism, for its drive to maximise production, and the authors emphasise the need to move towards maintaining a farming environment that also sustains wildlife. Such concern could hardly come at a worse time, when so many farmers have seen their incomes decline dramatically, yet throughout the land there are many who continue to carry out modest conservation work which they cannot really afford.

Of course we need to keep up the pressure on landowners to manage their estates in ways most sympathetic to wildlife, through hedgerow retention, sympathetic cropping regimes, minimising chemical use and so on, but there is still so much the rest of us can do.

We, too, must dig more deeply into our pockets. It's all very well to put peanuts in the back garden and join the RSPB, but how many of us, for example, are prepared to pay that often considerable premium for organically grown foods? Who is prepared to do without any chemicals in their own garden, and who is willing to buy trees, plants and shrubs which are specifically beneficial to birdlife yet not particularly attractive to us? In any event, for anyone who really cares for the nation's wildlife as a whole, there's not much point in creating cosy oases for a small number of garden species when over the fence lies a sea of increasing sterility.

While government is gradually being forced to take more notice of public concern for animals and plants, it is largely only through the magnificent efforts of our voluntary conservation organisations and a relatively small number of generous individuals and companies that much of our wildlife manages to cling on at all. Perhaps the new depth of interest in and concern for wildlife, not to mention man's own wellbeing, now demands far greater central allocation of government funds towards maintenance of a sustainable environment. Whatever our views, surely everyone should pay to save our natural heritage.

Some 60 years ago, the curator of my local museum wrote a book, *Nature Notes*, in which he stated, 'The bullfinch is a most unwelcome visitor to gardens. It comes from the woods in early spring when the fruit buds are swelling and strips tree after tree. Theobald examined the stomachs of 150 bullfinches and

'Numbers of bullfinches have fallen sharply, probably as a result of hedgerow loss and degradation.'

failed to find any evidence that they had eaten insects. House sparrows, chaffinches and greenfinches also occasionally attack buds but they also destroy large numbers of insect pests'. This typified the widespread hypocritical and uninformed attitude of earlier naturalists whose legacy still lingers.

I have been horrified that even in recent times bullfinches have continued to be legally killed in certain counties to safeguard fruit trees. Surely, in these highly inventive technological times there are better ways to protect trees. In any event, it is largely only when the bullfinch's most important natural foods – the seeds of ash, elm, bramble and dock – are insufficient to last through winter that the birds turn to eating buds in orchards. In the long run, if fruit growers helped to reinstate such trees and plants not only would they help themselves financially but also do much for the environment generally.

In my garden and on adjacent plots there are but a few apple trees and we always enjoy the sight of bullfinches. Sometimes the birds strip most of the buds, but we don't get over-excited because we can buy apples elsewhere. I suppose that, in a way, this is paying for conservation. A small price, yes, but many such actions could save a great many birds. ∎

Tailcorn

At least until the end of the 19th century a small Swedish town used to elect its mayor in a rather unusual way. All the contenders for the post were obliged to sit around a large round table. They lowered their heads until their beards were resting on the table. Then an official placed a flea in the middle of the table. When the flea hopped into a beard, that man was duly elected mayor.

Curious epitaphs

From the churchyard at Winterborn Steepleton, Dorset

Here lies the body Of Margaret Bent Who kicked up her heels And away she went.

Subscribe to The Countryman

– the perfect gift for yourself or a friend

The Countryman always gives you the true flavour of the country. It is written and illustrated by country people who tell of people and places, crafts and customs, wildlife and waysides that they know and love.

To savour that flavour eight times a year has never been easier. A subscription (all post and packing costs are included at no extra charge) is only £19.20 a year.

For yourself, for your friends and relatives near and far, *The Countryman* is a sure passport to the incomparable British countryside.

So subscribe now to 'the little green magazine', a unique publication whose arrival on one's doorstep has famously been described as like the arrival of a good friend.

To buy a subscription as a gift or for yourself, just turn the page and fill in the form.

FROM THE COUNTRYMAN TO YOUR HOME

A year's subscription (8 issues) costs £19.20 a year to any UK address; £23.30 (Europe by airmail or elsewhere in the world by surface) or £34.10 (rest of the world by airmail).

To: The Countryman Subscription Department, **FREEPOST** CY1061, HAYWARDS HEATH, SUSSEX RH16 3ZA.

Please send The Countryman for .... year(s)
❒ To me   ❒ To my friend/relative shown below

I would like a gift subscription to go to (leave this section blank if the subscription is for yourself):

Mr/Mrs/Miss/Ms ....Init................(BLOCK LETTERS)

Name...

Address..

....

Postcode...............................Country ....

My name and address is:

Mr/Mrs/Miss/Ms ....Init................(BLOCK LETTERS)

Name...

Address ....

....

Postcode ....Country ....

If you are buying a gift subscription only (ie not one for yourself) you must still fill in your own name and address. Subscription queries on 01444 445555

❒ I enclose a cheque/postal order for £.............. (pounds sterling) made payable to

IPC Magazines   OR

Please charge my: ❒ Visa   ❒ Mastercard   ❒ Amex   ❒ Diners

No: _ _ _ _ / _ _ _ _ / _ _ _ _ / _ _ _ _   Expiry date: _ _ _ _

Signature .... Date ....

In the USA and Canada a subscription costs $50. Contact The Countryman Subscriptions, 2039 Via Alexandra, Escondido, CA 92026, USA. IPC Magazines Ltd the publisher of The Countryman, may pass your name and address to other reputable companies whose products and services may be of interest to you.
Please tick this box if you prefer not to receive such offers. ❒   CM2

In search of the siskin

John Lawton Roberts on a lifetime's quest for one
of our most elusive birds

It began at Bevan's Pool, one of those deepenings of the middle Welsh Dee which at that time, in the mid-1960s, was still producing enough salmon to sustain a reputation. There, over the water, was what looked like a billow of smoke, but belied the appearance by giving out a strangely wheezy shimmer of sound. Drifting above the river, it drew itself into a thousand shapes before pouring into the crown of a single alder. Creeping closer and fingering my ancient binoculars, I saw to my joy that the tiny green birds – some with neat black caps and bibs – that hung upside-down on the new spring catkins, were siskins, a bird that until then I had seen only in illustrations in books.

This came at a watershed in my life. I had just been shamed out of the schoolboy 'egging' habit by my English master, a chain-smoking descendant of William Wordsworth. Learning of my robbery of a buzzard's nest he confronted me with the withering words: 'You've ruined their lives!' Chastened, I took down my electric train set from the attic and sold it for £14. This sum, magnified by a 'grant' from my father, transformed itself into a basic single-lens-reflex camera. A bird-photographer was born. And now the Siskin became his prime quarry.

At that time most photography of birds was done at the nest. This raised a problem, for my reading told me that siskins' nests, along with greenshanks' and grasshopper warblers', were among the most unfindable of all. The old egg-collectors had dubbed them 'blue riband' nests, for not only were they built at the tips of the highest branches of tall conifers, but their builders held a reputation for extreme elusiveness. Of a siskin at the nest, scarcely a photograph existed.

How different seemed those siskins that were increasingly visiting gardens at this time! There, unremittingly pugnacious towards birds twice their size, they amazed householders by their tameness, and puzzled scientists by their preference for the red variety of peanut-feeders. At first they were often reported as greenfinches. Soon, with their southward spread – fuelled by the maturing of the great post-war afforestations (siskins are a conifer species) – the birds became familiar late-winter guests, drawn to these free meals as natural foods became exhausted. Probably, also, the protein contained in peanuts helped bring the birds into breeding condition, as well as fuelling the return journey to the north where, reputedly, most of them still nested.

Year by year the flocks stayed on later, even into May or June. Then came proof of local breeding. On a June day I watched newly-fledged chicks; rotund, quivering balls of feathers, high on a plantation sitka, petulantly demanding food from their parents. From the British Trust for Ornithology had come a report of siskins nesting in a garden, in a hanging flower basket! But out of around 40,000 nest histories of British birds submitted annually on record cards to the Trust by volunteers, the average for siskins' nests was barely more than one. From Wales the only recent records were

of aborted attempts. I felt there must be a key, hitherto secret, to the finding of these nests.

In early 1990 it seemed to be in my hand, in the form of an ornithological paper on the timing of siskins' breeding. My hopes were premature. The authors, I found, had set up peanut feeders in Scottish forests, caught female siskins feeding there and judged their dates of laying from the state of development of their brood patches – the bare, breast patch that helps to warm their eggs. Not a nest had been found. I felt badly let down.

Judge, then, how I felt when a friend casually mentioned the siskins that had nested in a 12-foot cypress in his neighbour's garden. He'd forgotten to tell me!

None of our garden's siskins

Scanning tall conifers for the elusive nest of the siskin. This can lead to 'a severe cricking of the neck'.

Cock siskin on garden cherry in early spring. Peanuts supplied by man may help bring them into breeding condition.

seemed even to think about nesting. And in the moorland-edge plantations, in those years when flocks remained until mid-summer, time after time males would flutter and circle in shimmering display over clearings that perfectly matched the books' descriptions of ideal nesting habitat. The females, however, seemed to do nothing but feed. I gave up trying to let the birds lead me to the nests and instead tried 'cold searching', walking beneath the trees and scrutinising the tips of boughs for nest-shaped protuberances. Hours of this eccentric-looking activity turned up several chaffinches' nests, much frustration – and a severe cricking of the neck.

Suddenly, in 1998, everything changed. The previous breeding season in Scotland had been particularly productive, and droves of these birds were thought to have moved south, intent on breeding. By late March, three hen siskins in our garden were looking suspiciously broody. Their males were in constant, close attendance and on invitation – a chick-like quivering of the wings and open-mouthed begging – fed the hens with a mash of ground peanut. Then one hen, almost at my feet, pulled a strand of Shetland pony hair from the mud and flew far and straight to the top of a towering Douglas fir, all of 100ft from the ground. With binoculars I saw it enter a clump of needles right at the tip of the longest bough on the tree. Ten days later I noticed something hanging from the end of the branch. My telescope showed a soggy mess of hair and moss. The magpies, it seemed, had found the nest too.

As if this find had broken a spell, three more nests were soon found, the first only 20ft from the ground in a pine plantation seemingly full of

Siskin eggs: 'sky-blue, red-flecked' and a 'blue riband' find for the old egg-collectors.

siskins. Up went the scaffolding, topped by a hide. But oddity still reigned, for the well-feathered chicks were fed only by the male, a strikingly colourful bird 'like a canary', as my companion said. When the hen came to the nest, she merely plucked at its wool walls and ignored her begging chicks. We soon found the reason. Two pines away she was building a second nest.

There was more to learn. Watching from our hide, we found that the male fed his chicks twice as often on sunny, calm days as on cool ones. We traced the cause to the Scots pines whose seeds he was gathering – from cones that opened in the sun, but clammed so tight in cold weather that he could not extract their seeds. Whatever alternative food source he used was

A male siskin on a garden feeder. Siskins moved into the writer's garden in the 1960s, showing surprising tameness and a puzzling preference for red peanut feeders.

Hen siskin feeding her chicks on seeds. To photograph this species at the nest was the writer's ultimate ambition.

apparently far less productive.

We visited the plantation soon after the chicks fledged and were puzzled to find it all but siskin-less. The four sky-blue, red-flecked eggs, that 'our' hen had laid in her new nest were wet and deserted. We examined the cones on the pines and found them emptied of seed. Like us,

the hen siskin had not foreseen this collapse of the food supply. Rather than risk starvation, she had left her eggs and joined the search for an uncropped harvest.

The ancient law of the nomad had prevailed – and, in doing so, closed our brief window on the hidden half of the siskin's life. ∎

FOR A GOLF LOVER

Anyone who likes golf will love **The Man Who Inherited a Golf Course**. This super novel tells the story of Trevor Dukinfield who wakes up one morning to find that he is the owner of his very own golf club – fairways, bunkers, clubhouse and all. There's one snag: to keep the club he must win a golf match. And he's never played a round of golf in his life. *"The scenario is tailor made for Vernon Coleman's light and amusing anecdotes about country life and pursuits"* said the Sunday Independent. *"Very readable!"* said Golf World. *"Hugely enjoyable in the best tradition of British comic writing"* said the Evening Chronicle. *"The mix of anecdotes and moments of sheer farce make for an absorbing read"* said the Evening Telegraph. A terrific present for anyone who enjoys golf, and much more fun than another pair of socks! Only £12.95.

... A CAT LOVER

Alice's Diary tells, with great humour and insight, of a year in the life of a mixed tabby cat. Our files are bursting with letters from readers who love this book. *"Wonderful ... so beautifully written, it was a great pleasure to read"* wrote Mrs Y of Essex. *"Please send copies of Alice's Diary to the eleven friends on the accompanying list. It is a wonderful book which will give them all great pleasure,"* wrote Mr R of Lancashire. **Alice's Diary** is delightfully illustrated. A must for all animal lovers. Only £9.95.

... A CRICKET LOVER

The Perfect Present

Solve your present buying problems NOW by choosing from this selection of beautifully bound and jacketed hardback books from bestselling author

Vernon Coleman

"Vernon Coleman writes brilliant books" THE GOOD BOOK GUIDE

OUR GUARANTEE

If, for any reason, you are not happy with your books then simply return them to us in good condition within 28 days and you will be sent a full refund – no questions asked.

The Village Cricket Tour is a novel which describes the adventures and mishaps of a team of amateur cricketers who spend two weeks on a cricket tour of the West Country and which has been compared to Jerome K Jerome's classic "Three Men in a Boat". *"I enjoyed it immensely"* wrote Peter Tinniswood in Punch. *"He has succeeded in writing a book that will entertain, a book that will amuse and warm the cockles of tired hearts." "Coleman is a very funny writer,"* said This England. *"All the characters are here, woven together by a raft of anecdotes and reminiscences and a travelogue of some of the most picturesque spots in the south west."* A great gift for cricket lovers. £12.95.

To order send details of the books you would like, your name and address along with your cheque/PO (payable to Publishing House) to: **The Countryman, Sales Office CM17, Publishing House, Trinity Place, Barnstaple, Devon EX32 9HJ, England.** Post and packing is FREE in the UK (£1 per book Europe or £2 per book elsewhere). To pay by credit card please telephone our 24 hour orderline on 01271 328892 (this number may also be used for queries). We look forward to hearing from you.

Letters to the editor

Millennium truths

Dozens of readers have written taking Rusticus to task over when the new millennium actually starts ('Born-again writer' December 10, 1999 issue). All are of the opinion that we have been celebrating a year early. Here we publish extracts from four of those letters.

Sir, So Rusticus cannot understand why people state that the new millennium will not start until January 1, 2001. I will put forward the arguments as I understand them. They start from the fact that there was no year 'nought'.

The first year was number 1 AD and so the first century must cover the years 1 to 100 inclusive. The second century, therefore, had to run from years 101 to 200. We have to continue with this system, as no century can have 99 years, up to the present century which must therefore run from 1901 to 2000 inclusive and not, as erroneously thought, 1900 to 1999. The same arguments have to apply to millennia which run 1 to 1000, 1001 to 2000, 2001 to 3000 etc.

Richard Brooks,
Stourbridge, West Midlands

Sir, Rusticus is wrong in stating that the first year of any century starts at nought: 1 BC is followed immediately by 1 AD and the last year of that century must be 100 AD (not 99 AD), and so on.

The 'folk' who believe this include those at the Royal Observatory, and it has been accepted by the Millennium Commission and its spokesman Lord Falconer though he went on to justify, rather unconvincingly, the Commission's 'deliberate' mistake in celebrating in January 2000 by maintaining that we have to keep in line with the rest of the world.

Millicent Monck-Mason,
Ambleside, Cumbria

Sir, I was interested to read recently – I think in the *Daily Telegraph* – that the end of the 19th century and the beginning of the 20th were celebrated on December 31, 1900 (not 1899). Were people more educated then, or just less impatient?

I think the logical case for the current millennium having another year to run is beyond reasonable dispute, but I acknowledge having the figure 2 at the beginning of the year for the first time was a powerful temptation, and it was one to which our populist Government and others have succumbed.

D.K. Reid,
Weybridge, Surrey

Sir, I am sure many people would agree with me that the third millennium does indeed begin on January 1, 2001, but are quite happy to get the fuss over with a year early.

I have often thought how much easier it would be if there had been a year nought, because when I was growing up it took me some time to realise that the years 1501 to 1599, for example, were not the fifteenth century but the sixteenth!

Emily Tawse,
Oxted, Surrey

••••••••••••••••••••••••••••••••••

Giant cones

Sir, Jerome Betts, in his interesting article 'Cones can kill' (Dec 10, 1999), states that the coulter pine was named after the American botanist John Merle Coulter. I believe this to be wrong.

During March 1832 the Irish botanist, Dr Thomas Coulter, met David Douglas in California and invited him to accompany him on a cactus hunt to Colorado.

As Douglas was waiting for a Russia-bound ship to take him to Sitka in Alaska he declined the invitation. Coulter left him and returned during July with many specimens, and seed, and reports of a big-coned pine he had discovered in the Santa Lucia Mountains.

Douglas, who never saw the tree, sent the seed to Kew and the pine was named *Pinus coulteri* by D. Don in 1836. It is generally acknowledged that the name recognizes the Irish botanist.

Martyn Baguley,
Edinburgh

••••••••••••••••••••••••••••••••••

Living in tin

Sir, I was very interested in the article on tin tabernacles (Dec 10, 1999) because my grandmother used to live in one during the Second World War.

She had been bombed out of her London home and came to live with us in Hampshire, until she found this redundant tin tabernacle in Haslemere, Surrey. It was called Little St Cross.

She must have been in her late eighties when she moved in, but soon, and with help, she had transformed it into a beautiful, cosy little home. By the use of long, thick curtains she divided the space into three rooms. My memories are of a place glowing with colour, warmth and well-being. There were always snowy white lace curtains and crisply starched cotton curtains at the windows. Her furniture, copper and brass were polished and gleaming, and her handwoven linen and wool covers and cushions lent a richness to her rooms.

I was at a boarding school in Haslemere during part of the war and was allowed home some weekends. The school was three-quarters of a mile from granny's, up the hill. On Saturday mornings Mrs Fitzgerald, her helper, would arrive to fetch me and we would walk back down the hill to Little St Cross where lunch was waiting. Then it was down the hill to the bus stop and the hour's journey to the country lane bus stop where my mother would be waiting for me with my dog.

On Sundays I had to get the afternoon bus back to Haslemere. But tea at granny's, sitting round her cosy stove with freshly baked scones or muffins softened the return to school.

She continued to live at Little St Cross throughout the rest of the war, and for a year afterwards, until one day her helper found her on the floor of the kitchen – she had been baking scones and was in her 93rd year. It was the best way for granny to go, still independent in her own little home.

Shirley R. Dawson,
Ellesmere,
Shropshire

....

Leeches in the 1930s

Sir, I found the feature 'Blood letting and leeches' in the December 10, 1999 issue most interesting especially noting that each leech cost £10, a far cry from when I was an apprentice in a north London pharmacy in 1938. I was introduced to a tank of these black creatures and told that one of my duties was to look after them.

Saturday we worked until 9pm and that was when the chits used to come in from the many doctors around, requesting a leech price which was one shilling or 5p. I sorted out the small ointment box, cotton wool and one of my leeches, to send them on their journey.

After war service in the WRNS I went back to the pharmacy, alas tank empty, and soon medicine was changing; no longer ointments, tablets capsules being made to order, everything pre-packed.

Mrs V.W. Kingdon,
Ilfracombe,
Devon

Appalling farms

Sir, Humphrey Phelps' Country diary (October 29, 1999), went a long way to explaining a mystery I discovered on the Mendips in Somerset last spring.

While walking up a particular hillside, I noticed that pieces of lambs were strewn at intervals along the way and the next time I passed by they had been swept up. I wondered what had been their fate.

Last autumn found me there again with no flock in sight save for two ewes, quite separate from one another, in the last stages of dying. Both were old and thin, the first so weak it could scarcely stagger to lie under a hedge; the second blind and staggering in circles. When I did find the rest of the flock higher up, quite a number of lambs and ewes were so crippled as to almost avoid walking at any cost.

Obviously the farmer considered the sheep expendable and gave them little or no care. The farm I grew up on was something of a model I realise now in the face of intensive animal raising. Many current farming practices would cause howls of anguish from the farmers I once knew.

A.G.K. Berridge,
Bristol

....

Indian saw pit

Sir, I enjoyed the 'From the archives' photograph in your October 29, 1999 issue, of the men working in a saw pit. I have worked in agriculture and forestry since 1952 but have never seen a saw pit in use, though I have seen the remains of many when walking through beechwoods in the Chilterns.

You might be interested in the

Watching the trains

Sir, Like Nick Pigott (October 29, 1999) I too enjoy rural railways but with a difference. He looks back a third of a century to his days in short trousers; I can look back over two thirds of a century to watching the trains of the GNR and the LNWR crossing the Fosseway while sitting in my pram in the early 1920s! A few years later I enjoyed picking cowslips on the railway embankments which were kept clear of scrub and long grass by the fires caused by sparks from the engines. I don't think Mr Pigott's lobbying will get us back to that era.

In spite of all this nostalgia I have very few recollections of ever travelling on the trains in question; the journeys I did make I could still make today. Mr Pigott is making the mistake of assuming that country folk travel by bus because Dr Beeching closed their railways; in fact he closed the railways because they preferred to travel by bus! When the railways were built there were no buses and in the countryside the majority live quite a distance from the station.

Like historic houses, museums and country parks, rural railways are to be enjoyed rather than used as a convenient means of transport. As such we would all welcome their preservation but please remember that it was not in Dr

A cut above the rest: see 'Indian saw pit' (opposite).

photograph (above), taken in South India a year ago, of sawyers ripping some 150-year-old panel planks into two thinner (½in) panels for re-use in some alteration work.

They were craftsmen, moving from job to job and being paid by the piece, in this case 8 rupees per square foot (equivalent to about 12p per square foot) which gave them a comparatively good living provided their health remained good. Certainly there seemed to be no shortage of work for them – they were running a week or two late.

David Bourne,
Flaxton, York

Beeching's remit to provide an enjoyable pastime; his job was to give the country an efficient and economic transport system.

Mr Pigott should turn his attention to the mass of heavy transport on our roads. With the right pricing and taxation it would make sense for freight to go by rail.

Ian Rutherford,
Alderley Edge,
Cheshire

• •

Lamplighter

Sir, Regarding gas lamps in the August 13 issue. When I lived in Southampton in 1949 while in England on a teaching exchange, the lamplighter came along each evening on his bicycle with the pole slung under his seat along the bar to the handlebars, paused under the lights turned them on and then rode on.

Being an early bird I also watched him turn them off soon after daybreak. I was intrigued by this, to me, antiquated system.

Mrs A.M. Ingram,
Somerset West,
Republic of South Africa

Sir, Your recent correspondence on lamplighters reminds me of those wonderfully melancholy lines by T.S. Eliot:

And at the corner of the street a lonely
cabhorse steams and stamps,
And then the lighting of the lamps.
Ethel Tiptree,
Croydon

• •

Pound spotting

Sir, with reference to your article on village pounds (October 29, 1999). As your contributor said, these were essential prior to the widespread urbanisation of large areas of erstwhile countryside. I am familiar with the brick and planked pound in front of the Ring o' Bells pub just below West Bromwich old church.

The other, which I believe may be mediaeval and somehow under the aegis of the nearby church at Wolverley, Worcestershire, is cut out of the sandstone rock and has an iron door frame and door, with two small openings cut in the, I presume, wrought sheet.

Geoff Guise,
Quarry Bank, West Midlands

Sir, Your village pound piece re-kindled thoughts of an event in, I think the late 1940s. At the time, my late father was employed as head gardener at Tingehurst Manor in Buckinghamshire. This fact determined that we had to live in the gardener's cottage which was next to the village pound.

One morning I departed, hurriedly as usual, for work only to notice that a pig was enjoying some sleep, confined to the pound. I gave little thought to that fact during the day, but on my return home enquired of my father as to how the beast had been confined to the pound.

He endeavoured to explain that the pig had been placed in the pound during the hours of darkness. The funny part of the story was the fact that the pig had been confined to the pound by the gentleman who, on the following day, had to admit that he was the rightful owner of the beast.

E.A. Jackson,
Redruth,
Cornwall

Take-home pay

Sir, I found the closing item 'End of an era' in your Comment (December 10, 1999) most interesting. You mention the unprecedented changes that have taken place in rural Britain over the past 75 years. Well, very few of your readers, if any, have had those changes set before them more dramatically than I have.

In 1927, my father's take-home pay amounted to no more than £1 9s 2d a week (£1.46). That is all we – a family of six – had to live on. There were no perks, no government aid, no help whatsoever. Today, my son's take-home pay is approximately 666 times that amount. He had a top-class, state-aided education and, all credit to him, has put it to good use.

You were right in saying that we villagers were poor back in 1927. There was money only for bare essentials.

When my father, a skilled farmwork-er, decided to quit agriculture and try his hand labouring elsewhere for another £1 a week, he discovered he needed a bicycle in order to ensure that he got to work on time. He chose a Raleigh LR Popular at £7 14s – £1 deposit and 12 monthly payments of 11s 2d (I still have his payment card dated 30/5/27).

Initially, he could only scrape together half the deposit and had to borrow the rest from friends and neighbours; which meant that when the next payment was due, he not only had to find 11s 2d but also another 10s to repay the money he had borrowed earlier on.

I still remember the anxious moments my parents endured, and the stringent budgeting they practised to pay for dad's bike. Today, my son could buy any bicycle he fancied by just showing his credit card, and think nothing of it.

L.G. Scales,
Bishop's Stortford, Herts

Seals at risk

Britain plays host to half the world's population of grey seals, yet in some quarters they are very unpopular. Brian Martin reports

Britain's two species of seal – the grey and common – have both endured very stormy waters over the last century or so, and while the populations of both are on the up they remain at considerable risk on several fronts.

In the late 1800s grey seals were rare in British waters, but when they became our first mammal to be protected by legislation, in 1914, they started to make a sustained recovery. The Conservation of Seals Act (1970) strengthened their protection with a closed season from September 1 to December 31, and since 1960 their population has doubled to over 80,000 animals.

This is extremely good news as British waters host half the species' world population. However, such a dramatic increase in numbers has led to claims that seals have been causing great damage to fisheries. The mammals try to take salmon from fish farm nets in sea lochs and in doing so either damage the fish or tear the nets and allow valuable fish to escape. Many

Seal and pup: 'it is not surprising that there is a public outcry over the killing of such an appealing animal'.

David Kjaer

anglers, too, strongly resent seals, especially since the run of salmon has declined dramatically.

Recent research has suggested that the salmon does not appear to be a significant part of the grey seal's diet, but commercially important wild fish such as cod and herring are probably taken in large numbers. Furthermore, grey seals eat large numbers of sand eels, which are caught for use in fish meal but not for human consumption.

Grey seals are also said to be responsible for the large increase in parasites on wild fish such as cod and herring. But there is still much to discover about the relationship between numbers of seals and the incidence of fish parasite infestations.

In addition, the increased number of grey seals breeding on the Farne Islands have caused much soil erosion and concern for other local wildlife. As a result of all this, a number of organised grey seal culls have been undertaken, not to mention the unknown but potentially significant number of seals which may be killed quietly by individual, understandably aggrieved, fishermen. Unsurprisingly, the public outcry against any culling of such an appealing animal has been enormous.

Another major threat is disease, especially the recently discovered, so-called seal plague phocine distemper virus. Although only some 300 of the 3,000 seals which died in the 1988 outbreak were grey (the others being common seals), blood tests revealed that most grey seals had been exposed to the virus. By mid-1989 the virus had more or less disappeared and surviving seals were immune. Luckily, the immunity is inherited, but unfortunately such immunity is relatively short-lived, and of little use beyond the age of two years. As a result there is a real fear that a second major outbreak could occur if another vector appears.

The most popular theory is that the vector in the 1988 outbreak was the harp seal, which is a common carrier. Usually, this species is happy living further north, in the Barents Sea and other arctic waters. However, if fish stocks are short, harp seals must forage further afield, and it is thought that some which carried the virus ventured into British waters in 1988.

As worldwide over-fishing continues and global warming intensifies through mankind's careless and selfish activities, there is no doubt that both land and sea animals such as seals will be put at increasing risk. The more southerly foraging of harp seals could well become a regular occurrence, just as other species of land and sea mammal, insect and bird have already started to extend their ranges both north and south.

As seals are at the top of the food chain, they tend to accumulate pollutants such as heavy metals and polychlorinated biphenyls (PCBs) which are persistent in the environment. Thus seals feeding on fish with high levels of PCBs may fail to breed and pollution could significantly hinder recovery of populations reduced through disease.

Whether you like seals or loathe them, it's about time we started to behave much more responsibly and stopped treating our seas and oceans as gigantic dustbins. ∎

Lunching on pollution

Michelle Corps on a natural way to clean up the land

Tar-eating bugs? It sounds unlikely, but the use of bacteria to clean up pollution — known as bio-remediation – is now a reality. It's expensive, which is why it has only recently been tried here in Britain, but supermarket giants Tesco, in collaboration with Professor Nicholas Lepp and Robert Edwards of the John Moores University, have changed all that.

The Lanstar site in Liverpool was a tar distillery for more than a century. Before the bugs went to work it had been derelict since the early 1990s, the land severely contaminated, the site an eyesore. Now, due to a 'significant private investment' from Tesco, and the scientific know-how of the University's staff, the land will be cleaned up naturally – using micro-organisms that feed on what the scientists call persistent organic pollutants (POPs) – basically all kinds of industrial sludge, but especially oil.

The bugs will make the land clean enough to build on, which reduces the need to use rubbish tips such as landfill sites – and as more brownfield sites can be used for building, there will be less pressure to utilise greenfield land.

According to Professor Lepp – an expert on soil technology – tests on the soil revealed a strain of bacteria that had not previously been recognised, but that – incredibly – had evolved to feed on oil and toxic sludge. Based on these tests, the clean-up at Lanstar was carried out simply by encouraging the existing bacteria to multiply.

The site was first cleared of solid debris, then all the soil, of differing contamination levels, was thoroughly mixed to ensure that the pollution levels were even throughout – making it

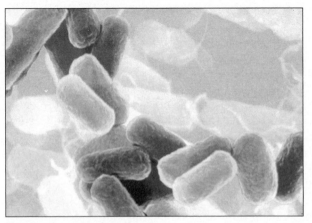

Bugs with a taste for oil.

The next step: Ash Road in Liverpool, which is soon to be cleared using the new 'superbug'.

easier for the bacteria to break down. Minerals were then applied to the soil to 'counteract the effects of heavy metals' which slow the bacteria.

Just enough oxygen, and organic nutrients such as nitrogen and phosphorus, were provided to feed the bacteria without making them dependent, while also creating optimum conditions for them to breed. It's a bit like adding fertiliser to your garden and turning the soil. After three to six months of regular feeding and turning, the level of contamination is, according to the experts 'significantly reduced'.

The beauty of this new venture is that the process is environmentally friendly as it uses only natural materials. As professor Lepp says, 'We are literally breathing new life into disused land'.

With luck, the success of these new superbugs will encourage other companies to use brownfield sites, rather than our dwindling, precious areas of countryside.

Digging round the country

Archaeological news from Francis Pryor

The Orkney Islands possess some of the most exciting archaeological sites to be found anywhere in Europe. One reason for this is that the local stone splits relatively easily into flat-sided slabs that are perfect for use in tombs and buildings. High quality timber is also hard to come by, so everything possible must be made from stone. Stone, of course, survives the passage of time very well – which is why there are so many ancient remains in Orkney.

Now archaeology is a very small profession. A recent survey of Britain estimated there were approximately 614 professional archaeological organisations, employing just 4,425 archaeologists. So it's hardly surprising that one frequently runs across old friends and colleagues doing new jobs in the most unexpected of places. Jane Downes, who is a lecturer at Orkney College, was once a key member of my own team at Flag Fen, but now she runs a survey of Orkney Barrows (burial mounds) for Historic Scotland, the government agency responsible for the historic environment in Scotland (English

Jane Downes

Within the small Bronze Age (2500-1500) burial mound at Linga Fiold, was a stone box or cist, containing the bones of two cremations, in the foreground, below the scale, is the lid of a pottery vessel.

Heritage and Cadw are its equivalents in England and Wales).

Barrows and other ancient earth-works are being damaged on Orkney and elsewhere by ploughing, and by other less obviously destructive forces, such as rabbits and cattle. As a response to these problems, Historic Scotland commissioned Jane and her team to investigate six Orcadian mounds. Nowadays it can sometimes take several years to fully excavate a barrow, but Jane's team were asked to undertake smaller scale investiga-tions, to establish the date of the mounds and the extent to which they were being damaged.

At the end of the excavations, three of the six mounds proved to be Bronze Age barrows (say 2,000-1,500 BC), all of which contained cists, or stone boxes in which cremations were placed. Some of these cists had been 'sealed' or signed-off with offerings of stone tools – plough points and mattock blades. In some cases the cists had been exposed and were actively being destroyed by rabbits – an animal that was introduced to Britain 3,000 years after the Early Bronze Age. One mound was Neolithic – perhaps 1,000 years earlier than the cist burials – and of the remaining two, one was modern and one was most probably a Viking period barrow.

The investigation of the six mounds was just a part of a larger Orkney Barrows Project, which Jane and her team have been working on since 1993. During that time they have vis-ited and recorded every surviving burial mound in the Orkneys. There were 700 known mounds at the start of the survey, but in the past few decades 150 of these had been destroyed and of the 550 remaining, 260 had been damaged. That's a terrible price that our children and grand-children must pay for 'progress'.

The Emperor Hadrian's great work

I won't pretend that I'm a great fan of the Romans, because I'm not. I have always believed that they exploited Britain and curbed our native genius. But having said that, the archaeologi-cal remains they left behind, after their relatively short stay in Britain (AD 43 to 410), are truly spectacular. And nothing is more spectacular than Hadrian's Wall which crosses some of the finest upland countryside in Europe. Many non-Roman tribes were keen to share some of the Empire's prosperity, with or without permission. So the great Wall was built across Northumberland, on the orders of the Emperor Hadrian, after his visit to Britain in AD 122.

If you visit this World Heritage Site you are struck by the remoteness of much of the Wall, especially those lengths that span the higher crags. If one looks at modern artists' reconstructions one is struck by the fact that the southern, Roman, side is neat and well tended moorland, whereas the land to the north is open, treeless, windswept and wild. But recent aerial photographs have revealed that, in point of fact, the landscape was very different. Far from being uncultivated moor, the countryside on both sides of the Wall was parcelled-up into walled and ditched fields, with clear evidence for 'cord rigg' – narrow ridges and furrows produced by digging over the ground with spades. In Ireland these ridges are known as 'lazy beds'.

Within the fields, again on either side of the Wall, are little farmsteads and yards for the animals, built by the native British population. This organised landscape refutes our minds' eye picture of a barbarian wilderness, butting up against the newly arrived forces of Classical Civilisation. Far from wild, this new view of the Wall seems almost suburban.

Last rites, Roman style

The recent discovery of a rich lady in a lead coffin in the Spitalfields Roman cemetery in London has caused great public interest. She was buried towards the close of the Roman period, in the fourth century AD. Her head lay on a pillow of bay leaves and her body was wrapped in at least two sheets of very fine cloth, decorated with gold threads. All this is by now well known. But Roman burials often included objects that were left outside the coffin, perhaps to be used by the dead person when their spirit moved out of the grave and into the Next World. I recall a child's coffin at Arrington, in Cambridgeshire, which had a set of miniature clay models – perhaps toys or guardian forces – outside it. Outside the coffin of the Spitalfields lady the excavators found a superb, decorated glass phial, which looked rather lie a narrow test-tube and with it was a jet rod, of the same length.

The Romans often included jet objects in graves. Presumably the phial held perfume or ointment which may have been spread on the lady's face or hair using the jet rod, at the last moment, before the lead coffin lid was sealed in place. It's the little details of this sort which help to bring the past to life. ∎

Small Bronze Age (2,500-1,500 BC) burial mound at Linga Fiold, in the Orkney Islands. The turf and topsoil have been removed to reveal a honey-comb of rabbit burrows.

Country characters

Humphrey Phelps remembers Arch Ayland, the carrier

Back in 1900, William Ayland was the village carrier and coalman. His son Alfred and grandson Arch continued in the same trades, except that they were called hauliers, not carriers. Alfred was a small man with a large drooping moustache who used to 'play the bones' at village concerts, and was a church bell ringer. He was very fond of a drop of whisky; whisky had once cured some illness that he'd had and perhaps that was why he took frequent drops as a constant precaution against a recurrence of the illness.

In the days when Alfred was active, beer and especially cider were comparatively cheap compared to a measure of whisky, and everyone fought shy of buying him a drink in the pub. Until one day a rough old farmer went into the village pub and saw Alfred drinking a mug of cider. 'I thought this was my chance to buy Alfred a drink without it costing me much,' he said later. 'So I said, "the same again for Mr Ayland." I was flabberghasted when I was asked for the money, I thought a mistake had been made and I didn't mince my words either. But I was told that I'd asked for the same again for Alfie, and that he was having double whiskies in his cider.'

When asked why he didn't take a holiday, Alfie replied, 'What do I want with holidays. I enjoy myself every day'.

Alfie's son, Arch, was not so small as his father, but even so he wasn't a big man, not in build although his heart was large. Everyone called him 'Arch' and everyone liked him; I never heard him speak ill of anyone and I don't suppose that he had an enemy in the world. A keen footballer, he played for the village team for several years. Both father and son had a lorry each which were used to deliver coal and for general haulage. For transport of cattle, 'tops' were fitted. Alfred's lorry with 'top' looked rather strange as it approached, like somebody with one shoulder thrust well forward.

Some farmers took advantage of Arch's good nature; on market day, instead of having cattle penned and ready for loading, they waited for Arch to come and help round them up from the fields. And round and round the fields Arch would run. It made him late for market on that day and on subsequent journeys there. Farmers grumbled about Arch; perhaps they blamed his driving if their animals didn't fetch a good price. But no one held it against him for long and, anyway, Arch never bothered about payment. Some farmers never received bills or requests for money from him. 'We don't bother about them we know are all right', Arch used to say, and he didn't like to be asked for accounts. I once asked for a bill and his wife very sternly said, 'I won't have poor Arch worried about bills and don't you dare ever to ask for one again'.

When he retired he must have been owed thousands, but Arch would not have known how much, any more than farmers would have known how much they owed. Whenever he delivered coal I always paid him for it and for a bit more on account. It was all I could do. I didn't want to incur the wrath of Mrs Ayland again. But I couldn't always do that.

Arch delivered coal at all hours of the day and night. Sometimes it was days, even weeks, before he would deliver coal to houses. Women used to grumble and say, 'When he does come, I'll give him a piece of my mind'. When he did deliver he always had a cheerful grin on his coal-blackened face and instead of giving him a piece of their mind housewives would give him a cup of tea. They all said the same: 'When he did come he was so nice, I couldn't be cross with him'. They were right: however much anyone might grumble behind his back about his tardiness – face to face it was impossible to be cross with him.

At haymaking time he sometimes came with his lorry and a gang of men to haul bales from the field – Arch could always get help when he needed it, even to drive his lorry on Saturday market days when he was playing football. For haymaking, cider had to be provided; cider before we all went out to the field, cider when the lorry was loaded, cider back at the barn and cider when the lorry was unloaded.

Arch was wedded to that old lorry. Wherever he went he drove the lorry. Once they were going to a wedding a

'Arch delivered coal at all hours of the day and night...'

hundred or more miles away. 'How are you going to get there?' we all asked. 'In the lorry, of course,' said Arch, grinning and tugging at the lobe of his right ear – this was a regular thing, tugging at his ear. But his wife had a different idea. 'If Arch thinks I'm going to a wedding in that old lorry, he can think again.'

I was away when I heard that Arch had sold his lorry and business and bought a sporty little car. I admit I was shocked. The people I was staying with said that I was greatly upset by the news, and so I was – Arch without his lorry, what were things coming to.

Some years earlier he'd become a keen vegetable gardener, although I could remember the time when he wasn't. During the war I'd seen Mrs Ayland trudging along to the allotments with spade, hoe and rake, 'Arch' she said, 'won't put a spade in the garden'. When he was converted, he turned a drained mill-pond adjacent to his house into a garden, as well as cultivating ground at the back of his house. He'd haul manure from miles away if he saw some in a heap that he fancied – no one could refuse Arch. Runner beans were his speciality; he grew rows and rows of them. In fact he was quite fanatical about them and when his first beans were setting he became almost mawkish. 'I've got a bean this long,' he'd say with a silly look on his face as he extended thumb and forefinger to indicate its size. And when he had beans to pick and sell, his joy knew no bounds and if he had some particularly long beans he became ecstatic.

In his retirement he took to cider-making. He and an old friend, who had cider-making equipment, would travel miles for cider fruit – not just any old apples, not even any cider apples, but only the best, such as Kingston Black. I'd see that sporty little car go by, loaded with bags of apples, in the boot and on the roof, and Arch and friend grinning and as happy as Larry. The two of them had happy days making the cider and happy days drinking it. They made enough to last a year or more, and what's more they were very generous with it and it was excellent cider too. ∎

'In his retirement he took to cider making. He and an old friend... would travel miles for cider fruit.'

Brian Walker

The cycle of life

Stefan Buczacki on destruction, creation and garden design

Now here's a conundrum for a wet afternoon. Who spoke of 'that weeping gloom of March and April, that bitter blast outraging the honour of May – how often has it robbed me of heart and hope?'

No, I couldn't remember either, (although a quick check now reveals that it was George Gissing), but it was a sentiment to which I felt very close as I stood in a West Country gale a few weeks ago and watched large pieces of ancient oaks and cedars crashing to the ground around me. I could only feel relieved that they were not my trees and merely express sympathy with their owner.

Fortunately, he was a sanguine old soul who felt that he had seen much of it before in his 78 years; and fortunate too in that his land was extensive enough to take the loss without being totally denuded. But what impressed me most about the old boy's reaction was that he could see something that must be so hard for those in his situation to appreciate; that we were merely witnessing another facet of the cycle of life.

For those fallen branches and upturned roots will be manna to many small creatures and to things of even lowlier life form. The debris will provide them with places to hide and with food for months.

Of course, in a garden or other relatively ordered situation, the bulk of the timber will be cleared away and shredded or burned. And stumps too will be ground down, a task of some importance if honey fungus is to be dissuaded from making its presence felt in previously uncontaminated soil. But in the more rural places, I do hope that a proportion of the fallen timber will be allowed to remain, to provide places for insects, fungi, ferns and mosses to flourish.

It is commonly forgotten that some of the areas that have been spared the gales of recent years nonetheless suffered even more prodigious loss of trees when elm disease swept across the landscape in the 1970s. In my own county of Warwickshire and nearby Gloucestershire, there are many instances of once scarce creatures, fungi and lower plants becoming common as they flourished on the fallen elms.

But I am often asked about the value of what I shall loosely call 'tree waste' for general garden use. Can bark, sawdust or wood shavings serve any valuable purpose as mulch, soil amendment or nutrient?

The short answer is yes, of course; there is no organic matter that cannot find some useful purpose in the garden. And you may think, with commercially prepared and bagged bark at a price beyond the reach of many of us, that purpose must surely be a very precious one. In a sense, it certainly is a precious purpose, for tree products are renewable resources, especially when they are derived from deliberately cropped softwoods. And thus they provide a welcome change from the exploitation of non-renewable peat.

But what particular attributes do they have? Certainly not much in the manner of plant nutrient – the nitrogen content is only about 0.2 per cent while the phosphate and potash is scarcely measurable.

It is as simple organic bulk that tree products find their value, helping with other organic matter to improve soil structure and maintain its moisture content. But they will only achieve this satisfactorily after they have been composted. For if wood waste is added directly to garden soil, it will temporarily deplete the nitrogen content as it begins to decompose and may contribute some toxic substances that composting will allow to degrade or leach away.

If you read rather smart books on garden design, you will see further suggestions for the use of waste or even manufactured timber products in your garden. You will see that they can be used to produce step-ping places across beds of gravel or lawns. They can form the surfaces of whole patio areas or bridges over tiny streams. But only in smart garden design books they can, for I urge you not to be tempted into such silly ways unless turning your garden into a skating rink every time it rains is the objective. But used as edging or restraining material, timber is undoubtedly useful and relatively inexpensive.

I find it has a particular merit for confining gravel or even large bark chips that make the basis of informal paths. Use half round farm fence timber which is relatively cheap, give it an extra coat of preservative and anchor it with pairs of hard wood pegs hammered into the ground to produce something really durable yet attractively functional.

But let us return briefly to where I began and urge you, if you lose a tree, to think carefully about its replacement. In rural areas, the chances are that the tree will be a native species and I would like to think that it is with similar types they will be replaced. In more urban situations of course, it may well be that the existence of such trees had become unrealistic, their survival in the midst of human activity an anachronism of some well meant tree preserving legislation.

Then, of course, a smaller exotic, more suited to the urban environment would be appropriate. But do choose carefully and check on final heights and spreads.

Fallen timber will 'provide places for insects, fungi, ferns and mosses to flourish'.

CHRISTIE'S

FREDERIC, LORD LEIGHTON, P.R.A.
(BRITISH, 1830–1896)
Kittens
oil on canvas, 47 x 31 in. (119.4 x 78.8 cm.)
Sold at Christie's in June 1998

Fine Art Security Services

Fine Art Security Services Ltd.
42 Ponton Road
Nine Elms
London SW8 5BA
Tel: (020) 7622 0609
Fax: (020) 7978 2073

www.christies.com

Peace of Mind
High security storage for your property, either
for short or long term periods at our purpose-built
facility in Central London. Whether for single items
or complete collections, our unique services include
100,000 square feet of high-security storage, fully-
trained staff and highly competitive insurance rates.
You may qualify for our free collection service.
For peace of mind there is only one choice.
Please contact Richard Ellis on (020) 7622 0609.

Down among the dumplings

Jerome Betts on the virtues of a 'fair round belly'

The ink and wash caricature that accompanies this feature is dated September 12, 1791. It's title, 'A Natural Crop: alias A Norfolk Dumpling', may not mean much to the modern reader, but the expression 'A Norfolk dumpling' has been in use at least since Elizabethan times.

A pamphlet of about 1600, *The Beggar of Bednall Green*, refers to a man being surprised by his landlady when he was 'as naked as your Norfolk Dumplin', and another of 1608 mentions a man who 'lookt like a Norfolke dumpling, thicke and short'. However, in 1662, Fuller's *Worthies of England* explained the term a little more diplomatically. 'This cannot be verified of any dwarfish stature of people in this county... but it relates to the fare they commonly feed on.'

Those savoury boiled or baked globules of suet and flour were also known as 'pot-balls' in Norfolk, and more recently as 'swimmers'.

The Tatler told its readers in 1709 that 'An Esquire of Norfolk eats Two Pounds of Dumplin every Meal', which would seem enough to account for a 'Natural Crop' carrying all before him.

The physician and wit John

A Norfolk Dumpling: the expression has been in use since Elizabethan times.

Arbuthnot asked in his *Learned Dissertation on Dumpling* of 1726 'Why should Dumpling-Eating be ridicul'd, or Dumpling-Eaters derided?' Why indeed, except for the inevitable corpulence of two-pounds-at-every-meal consumers, or the rotund overtones of the word itself? It is, apparently, a diminutive of 'dump', in the sense of 'a small round object'.

The only other county, as far as I know, with which the transferred 'short and fat' meaning of dumpling is associated, is Devon, though to a much lesser extent.

There is certainly a popular Torquay pub, converted from a farm in 1951, called 'The Devon Dumpling', but the reason for this seems not to have been recorded. Its current eye-catching sign has a rather unusual interpretation of dumplings, Devonian or otherwise, as it shows the upper half of a well-developed serving-wench whose low-cut dress leaves little to the imagination.

It is possible the pub-christener was thinking of the poet John Wolcot, who produced satirical verses under the name Peter Pindar, and came from Kingsbridge in the extreme south of Devon. He wrote in 1816 of 'A servant of Sir Francis Drake... a true Devonshire dumplin'. The term was also defined in 1902 as 'a short, thick and plump young woman'.

Among other proverbial tags from the eastern side of England are 'Essex calves' and 'Cambridgeshire camels', the latter said to have originated in the old use of stilts to get around in the Fens.

Norfolk's epithet may sound a little squat and sluggish in comparison, but, in the days before the fitness mania dictated a slim outline before everything else, a 'fair round belly', as with the contemporary figure of John Bull, was regarded as a mark of affluence appropriate to the middle-aged.

So the lack of a lean and hungry look might after all have been intended as a kind of compliment to that top-booted, buff and blue N. Crop Esquire. Perhaps the proprietors of 'The Norfolk Dumpling', a restaurant in the live-stock market at Norwich, should consider him for their logo?

Curious epitaphs

From a gravestone in Leamington:
Here lies a miser who lived for himself,
who cared for nothing but gathering wealth.
Now where he is and how he fares,
Nobody knows and nobody cares.

Secrets of
The Garden House

Stuart Fraser reveals the history behind a little-known historic garden

T oday it is a gentle ruin, its soft walls the quiet centrepiece of a terraced, walled garden regarded as one of the finest in Britain. Surrounded by exuberant colours and extravagant, innovative planting, creating a quiet corner of beauty and tranquillity, it is hard to imagine this gardener's heaven as the eye of a storm – but that's how it could be described. For time is a tricky business at The Garden House: the romantic ruin sits quietly on a boundary between an exciting future based on a revolution in gardening techniques, and a dramatic past that is only now beginning to come to light. That past is unknown to most visitors to The Garden House.

The glorious 11-acre site on the edge of Dartmoor is open between March 1 and October 1, and overlooks the beautiful South Devon Lovecombe

Keith Wiley, Head Gardener at The Garden House, in the lime tree avenue: Amos Crymes planted a tree for each of his children.

Valley in the parish of Buckland Monachorum. The National Trust's Buckland Abbey, the home of the great Elizabethan seadog Sir Francis Drake, is close by.

To the visitor, The Garden House is the creation of two men: Etonian schoolmaster the late Lionel Fortescue, who came here in 1945 and created the walled garden; and his successor Keith Wiley, who is expanding the gardens in extraordinary style beyond the old stone walls.

But its story goes much further back, and research is now beginning to reveal the hidden past of The Garden House. The ruin at the heart of the estate is that of a vicarage dating back to the 14th century: here the priests of the Church of St Andrew in Buckland Monachorum created their grand residence. The vicars of Buckland Monachorum were a fascinating lot: the first to come to light is the remarkable Reverend Amos Crymes, incumbent between 1752 and 1783 – and the last priest to inhabit the old vicarage before it was pulled down and replaced by a mansion further up the hill which, today, partly functions as The Garden House's tea-rooms.

His lovely legacy is the lime tree avenue between The Garden House and the parish church. Amos planted one tree for each of the 15 children his wife Elizabeth bore him. Poor Elizabeth produced the children between 1750 and 1770 – when she died at the age of 42 soon after giving birth to the youngest child, George.

It is tempting to imagine Amos and Elizabeth making their yearly pilgrimage with a fresh young sapling to add to the avenue created for their children. Today, the lime trees – eight survive in rude health – are lovingly cared for by Keith.

He said: 'They are absolutely wonderful trees. The area is still known as 'Ten Trees' – we know that only ten of the Crymes' children survived to adulthood and I wonder if trees were planted for the five children who died, and then removed.'

There are now plans to put up a memorial to Amos, Elizabeth and their children – the inspiration of the lime tree avenue that frames, in the middle distance, the Church of which Amos was priest.

Continued on page 48.

The Church of St Andrew, where Amos Crymes was vicar from 1752 until 1783.

Continued from page 46.

A view of the gardens with the Church of Buckland Monachorum in the distance.

But he was, at first anyway, a reluctant man of the cloth. Much of what we know about him comes from the researches of Philip A. Crimes into his family history, which resulted in a book called *C(h)rymes* or *C (h) r i m e s .* Further work on the history of the vicarage has been carried out by local historian Tamsyn Blaikie.

Philip Crimes, a Londoner, describes how Amos was a member of the Crymes family that owned the vast Crapstone estates and held the living of Buckland Monachorum. His forefather Ellis, a humble London haberdasher, had bought the estate formerly owned by Buckland Abbey after the dissolution of the monasteries (the last Abbot of Buckfast later became vicar of Buckland Monachorum, living in The Garden House ruin).

But by 1744, when Amos became heir to the Crymes lands at the death of his 12-year-old brother Elizeus, the family fortunes were on the wane and the estate was heavily mortgaged. Amos was a minor, and it seems the trustees of his financially troubled estates, led by his great-aunt Sarah, decreed the boy go into the priesthood to provide him with a secure future.

But another trustee, Henry Warne, described young Amos as idle and having an aversion to learning, complaining that he had spent the better part of a year playing truant from school to follow hunting and other country sports. One of Warne's servants, Joan Dearing, said Amos

Autumn at The Garden House: a glorious 11-acre site on the edge of Dartmoor.

often declared his disgust at the idea of becoming a clergyman, saying he would rather do anything else. But other schoolmasters praised Amos's diligence, and by 1748 the 'idle' boy with an 'aversion to learning' was a student of Exeter College, Oxford. There he met Elizabeth Shilfox, and the couple married in April 1749. A year later, presumably crippled by debt and ongoing costly legal action surrounding the Crapstone estates and now of an age to make his own decisions, Amos sold the family lands, manor house and all.

Today, Crapstone Barton still exists – a lovely manor with a 1646 coat of arms above the grand fireplace in the great hall bearing witness to the last extension work carried out by the Crymes family – as squires of the parish, they threw the vicar out of The Garden House vicarage while building work was taking place, and temporarily took up residence there.

Amos came back to Buckland Monachorum in 1762, not as lord of the manor and not to grand Crapstone Barton, but as parish priest. Not that the vicarage was a humble residence.

Surviving accounts describe the home Amos would have inhabited; of three stories, stone-built with a slate roof, it had an oak-panelled parlour on the ground floor, a hall, a buttery, kitchen, beerhouse and cellar. On the first floor were four bedrooms and a study with fir-timbered floor and ceilings, and above were three more bedrooms and another room, again fir-timbered.

The couple must have needed the space: their first son, Amos, arrived in 1750 to be followed by Eliz (September 1751), Elizeus (August 1752), Emblem (August 1754), John (October 1755), Francis (May 1757), Lawrence (November 1758), Mary (November 1759), Honour (January 1761), Ann (December 1761), James (February 1763), Jane (May 1764), Elizeus (June 1765), Margaret (February 1769) and George (July 1770).

It was perhaps fortunate that the duties of a parish priest in the 18th century were light according to Philip Crimes: a few communions a year, the occasional sermon, ministering to the sick, baptisms, marriages and funerals. Amos held 70 weddings during his incumbency, fewer than three a year. He introduced the then trendy new fad of singers and a band in church in 1753 (at a cost of £6 a year), and later supervised the re-hanging of the bells. The couple and their growing family had a comfortable stipend of £120 a year – plus the income from the vicar's 52 acres of 'glebe'. ∎

The walled garden at The Garden House. In the background the ruins of the old vicarage where Amos lived.

Country notes

Robin Page on Lark Rise Farm and bringing back the birds

In many ways this has been one of the strangest winters that I can remember. It started late, and in fact it hardly started at all. On our heavy land our cattle were out in the meadows until well into November; usually by the middle of October they are in the yards for the winter.

Wet, clay and cattle are not good winter companions and if they were not brought inside, the fields would turn into a sea of mud. By bringing them in so late it meant that we saved a month's straw and hay, which in turn saved a month of manual work, as we still use small bales which have to be carried and broken up around the yards. I suppose that is one of the advantages of global warming, that it will make our livestock farming easier; the disadvantages and the consequences from them, on the other hand, do not bear thinking about.

Since the cattle came in we have had rain but the grass has never stopped growing and there was even a stunted hogweed in flower in February. At no time either, have I felt cold. My longjohns have remained carefully folded in the cupboard and I have worn gloves about twice. Now I know I have a certain amount of natural insulation these days, but I actually like the cold and I have missed it.

The saddest aspect of all this is that there has been no skating; my speed skates are hanging up untouched and I have not ventured into the Fens once looking for ice. What with global warming, health and safety and computer games, it seems to me that outdoor winter skating is doomed – another wonderful country tradition gone. I can only hope that in the pause between writing this article and its appearance in *The Countryman*, the weather experiences a dramatic change and my skates have been on overtime.

In my non-medical view too, it has been the lack of cold that has bred the flu epidemic. Warm weather always did bode ill, hence 'grass growing in January means a full churchyard'. In these parts there has almost been a queue to leave the planet. Fortunately my flu jab did the trick this year and I have had one of my most healthy winters ever – apart from my gently expanding natural insulation.

The other problem with the winter has undoubtedly been Tony Blair. The object of this column is not to be political, but I, like many other people welcomed his arrival in the top job in 1997. It felt like a good time for change and Labour certainly talked a good, happy, healthy, prosperous and environmentally friendly countryside when they were in opposition. Sadly, once in power they have whistled a different tune – with the countryside in crisis, socially, economically and environmentally.

It is odd. The only people doing well out of farming at the moment are those who run their farms very intensively, like factories. Farming to them is simply a food production process – to grow their crops as cheaply as possible, and make as much profit as possible, regardless of the environmental consequences or what happens to the wildlife that once shared the land with them.

On top of this there is also a new class of rural spiv – the farmer or landowner who joins the current get-rich-quick syndrome. With development out of control in southern England, they sell their farmyards and the meadows around them for development and in return they pocket cheques containing many noughts. In the last three years we have had five such offers for our farmyard near Cambridge; we have turned them all down. For me it would be like collecting 30 pieces of silver.

But amid the doom and gloom comes some very good news. On the land owned by the Countryside Restoration Trust (CRT), between the villages of Grantchester and Barton in Cambridgeshire, remarkable progress has been made and it is giving a message of hope for the future, if only the politicians would look, learn and listen. Two years ago, with help from the Heritage Lottery Fund, the CRT bought 140 acres of typical Cambridgeshire prairie, right next to the land it already owned. It bought it as part of its Sir Laurens van der Post Memorial Appeal, and called it Lark Rise Farm. For the first year it was still farmed in an intensive, prairie-like way, but last year we changed the system.

The land came under two government funded 'agri-environment' schemes – the Countryside Stewardship Scheme and the Arable Stewardship Pilot Scheme. Under these arrangements, instead of simply getting subsidies for production, the CRT's grants and subsidies have been linked to the environmental work being undertaken on the land. With the enthusiastic help of the tenant farmer, Tim Scott, and numerous volunteers the dead land has been transformed. With grass margins, beetle banks, newly planted hedgerows and wildlife strips, birds animals and insects have been given

'Along the scrub by a ditch were at least 30 reed buntings...'.

David Kjaer

the habitat they need for survival – and they like it.

In addition to this the CRT now receives financial help for growing spring crops. This means that we can leave winter stubble, and the birds and hares love that too. The other day I showed a journalist around the land and I was almost embarrassed by the amount of wildlife we saw – it was incredible: along the scrub by a ditch were at least 30 reed buntings and the stubble itself was alive with both skylarks and corn buntings. French partridges and pheasants were ten a penny and we saw at least three coveys of English partridges, one numbering 20 birds. To have seen so many English partridges on such a small area, in such a short space of time was remarkable and showed an astonishing shift of fortune for this wonderful symbol of a healthy countryside.

The CRT has numerous volunteer helpers and monitors. One of them is Bob Scott, once head of the RSPB's reserves management team. He is encouraged by what is happening and believes that already the CRT has the highest density of skylarks in Cambridgeshire.

But Lark Rise Farm represents even more – it is producing quality food and it is farming at a profit. Each year, the guru of agricultural economics, Professor John Nix, produces profit figures for farming according to market prices and costs. This year Tim Scott exceeded Nix's figures for three crops out of five.

This was a remarkable achievement for it shows that if given the opportunity, farmers could farm in an environmentally friendly way and they could survive financially if all the production subsidies were changed to environmental subsidies. At Lark Rise Farm we have shown that wildlife can be brought back and our tenant farmer can make a living. There is a hitch however. At the moment only two per cent of farming subsidies go into agri-environment schemes. ■

From the archives . . .

A woman churning butter talks to a milkman wearing a yoke to carry his pails. The photographer was William Grundy, whose wonderfully evocative pictures of rural Britain at the end of the 19th century are now part of the Hulton Getty collection.

A rag-bag of recipes

H. J. Mason on how to make a pigeon into a grouse

Irecently had the good fortune to come across an extraordinary old book which revealed a number of fascinating household tips. Well-thumbed – and already in its 14th edition when published in 1922 – it was obviously a popular choice for the time.

The author, L. Sykes, had collected recipes during the 19th century and given them the title *Olio*. She explained the word as 'a mixture or medley or collection' and quoted a reference to it in Samuel Pepys' diary. On April 5 1664, he wrote: 'At noon by appointment comes Mr Sheres... and we to the Mulberry Garden where Mr Sheres is to treat us with a Spanish Olio... and the Olio was indeed a noble dish such as I never saw better or any more of'. Mulberry Garden was a place of public entertainment on the site of which Buckingham Palace now stands.

Ms Sykes hoped that this distinctive title adequately expressed the character of the book as 'herein will be found recipes, not only for cookery, but for practically every known household requirement'. The author then begins to wax lyrical:

'Now ladies young and old
Be wise and use this book
For men will e'er think less of gold
Than of a dainty cook.

We've meat and fish and soup
 and jam
And care for tender feet
We've potatoes and roasted ham
And how to clean our teeth'.

Her recipe for Olio, 'a Spanish dish' suggests that the reader: 'Brown a trussed chicken in a little hot butter, drain it, place in a saucepan with 1.5lb of mutton, 1.5lb veal, and 1lb of steak, all previously browned. Add 1lb of streaky bacon, and cover with boiling water. Simmer gently for 1 hour, add half a head of celery with a bunch of parsley, 12 small onions, 6 small carrots and turnips. Boil gently until the vegetables are cooked. Season with salt and pepper. Place meat with vegetables around. Enough for 12 persons'.

If this is the recipe that Mr Sheres' cook was using, it is not surprising that Pepys thought it was a 'noble dish'. It is a pity that there is no indication of the size of pot or saucepan needed.

Much emphasis is put on seasonal cooking, both of meat – pork from September to April, veal from February to Autumn, mutton and Canterbury lamb all the year round but English lamb only from April to September – and of vegetables and fruit, most of which would have been grown in the kitchen garden.

Most of the recipes are modest both in the quantity and quality of the ingredients: 'Cheap soup can be made from 1 large onion, 1 turnip, 1 tablespoonful of cornflour, 1 quart (2 pints) of milk, and 3oz butter. Economy soup can be made from any scraps of vegetables, cooked or uncooked, any vegetable peelings (well washed) outer leaves of celery and other vegetables (not decayed) bacon and cheese rind (washed), a small bunch of herbs, pepper and salt.'

In contrast, the recipe for Olio soup, described as 'too extravagant and rich for the present days', was as follows: '7lb beef, and 6lb veal cut into small pieces and laid side by side in a deep pan and upon this a thin layer of suet and upon the top of that 4 onions cut into slices. Over the whole is poured a pint of water. The pan is placed in the oven and allowed to stand for two hours. Then the pan is half filled with water and allowed to boil gently, the scum being taken off continually. After two hours more, add half a leg of mutton, half a hare or rabbit, 2 old chickens, 2 old partridges, all cut up, besides celery, parsley, roots, cabbage, turnips and carrots also cut into slices. The pan is filled to the brim with water and allowed to boil for five hours'. Again there is no indication of the size of the pan needed nor is there any idea of the number of servings which would be produced.

Another recipe, with economy in mind, is for imitation grouse: 'Place half a red herring into the inside of a cleaned pigeon, roast in the usual way, basting well, take out red herring before serving'.

While the main part of the book is filled with cookery recipes, there are also numerous 'Wrinkles for the cook, and household hints'.

In the kitchen

'In private draw your poultry, clean your tripe,
And from your eels the string substance wipe,
Let noisome offices be done at night,
For they who like the meat abhor the sight.'

To catch fleas in bed

'Remove the bedclothes gently. Take a piece of damp soap and dab onto the flea. This prevents it from escaping'. I would have thought that the flea would long have disappeared before the soap could be applied!

There was no escape for moths. If they were 'in a carpet, spread a damp towel over the part and iron it dry with a hot iron. The heat and the steam kill the worms and the eggs'.

Economy returns in the use of an old mackintosh. 'Cut out the sleeves, turn it back to front, shape out round the neck, and use it back to front as an overall for washing up etc'. The 'use once and throw away' philosophy of today would have been regarded as a scandalous waste by our grandparents. But over two generations some things have changed very little; the hint for cleaning windows was 'make a wad of newspapers, moisten slightly with methylated spirits and polish with a moist duster. Add a very little methylated spirits to the water as this eases the process and helps to keep it clean longer'.

Methylated spirits is still widely used for this purpose.

The remedy for a swallowed wasp seems rather drastic. 'Immediately hold in the mouth a teaspoonful of salt. The salt will kill the wasp and help to heal the sting', assuming of course that the salt is readily available.

To catch wasps
'He hath found an old bottle, I cannot say where,
He hath bound it with skill to the back of a chair,
Fill of mild ale so balmy and sugar so brown,
and he'll trap them by dozens I'll bet you a crown'.

Early 19th century kitchen: recipes from this period invariably demand huge quantities of ingredients.

Undoubtedly as effective then as it is today.

In days when chickens roamed the farmyard, nests had to be hunted for in haystacks, barns and every nook and cranny. As there was no certainty how fresh the eggs were, it was important to know how to tell the age of an egg. 'Put into a glass of water. When fresh, the egg will sink to the bottom; when three weeks old the egg will be nearly on its side, broad end up; at three months old, it will stand straight up, the wide end first showing, and when very stale it will rise much higher above the water.'

Nothing was wasted in the kitchen. For instance, 'Put rotten apples into a stained aluminium pan, cover with water and bring to the boil. The stain will be removed'. Great care must have been needed to avoid a conflagration when applying this recipe 'to arrest falling hair'. 'Rub with neat's foot, or coconut oil, and petrol, using the petrol every day and the oil three times a week. (Avoid a fire or an uncovered light.)

Finally...

'I wish you good health,
For you cannot deny,
That health is a treasure
Which gold cannot buy.'

THE PERFECT GIFT

a subscription to **THE COUNTRYMAN**

One full year (8 issues) for just: £19.20

(Europe and Eire by surface: £23.30
Airmail/rest of the world by air: £34.10)
I enclose a cheque for £ ....
for a year's subscription (8 issues) **OR** please charge my
ACCESS/VISA

Card number: ....

Expiry date: ....

Please send magazines to:
(please **print** and use the **postcode**)

Mr/Mrs/Miss/Ms..Init............
Surname...
Address:...
....
Postcode...............................Country...............................

Cardholder's name and address if different from above:
(please **print** and use the **postcode**)

Name: ....
Address:...
....
....
....

DIAL A SUBSCRIPTION ON
01444 445555, or for credit cards 01622 778778

Or send your completed cheque to:

Countryman Subscriptions,**FREEPOST CY1061,
Haywards Heath, Sussex RH16 3ZA**

CM2

SUBSCRIPTIONS ORDER FORM

A nest under the waves

Leslie Jackman among the sticklebacks

It was a day in late spring. Wandering among the low tide rock-pools, I spotted movement among a clump of red seaweeds. After a patient wait, it turned out to be a 15-spined stickleback, and a very busy stickleback at that.

Bear in mind the fact that the pool was little larger than the average kitchen table. And what happened within that space became more remarkable as I watched. The 7in-long fish was nest building and some of the structure was already in place.

The nest – about the size of a tennis ball – was being built among the fronds of *Cystoseira* (no common English name, I fear). The little fish was busy plucking mouthfuls of a red seaweed and carrying it across the pool. Sensitively, yet deliberately, it then pushed the pieces into the developing ball nest.

Nest of 15-spined stickleback woven into Cystoseira.

Unfortunately, just as it began to get really interesting, the flood tide drove me back up the shore.

Hardly believing it might still be there next afternoon, I returned. Sometime during the past night and morning that nest had been transformed into a tightly inter-meshed ball. And the little fish was resting nearby. Unable to go back to the shore for two days, it was late afternoon when I took a third look.

It was almost impossible to believe my eyes. That little fish had bound the entire structure in a network of filaments similar to thick monofilament fishing line. It was obvious this thread ensured the survival of the nest in rough seas. It was much later I discovered that the male nest builder secretes this gelatinous, thread-like material from its body to bind the seaweed in place by swimming round and round the nest.

During a final visit I noticed a large number of white, pea-sized globules attached to seaweeds in various directions up to two yards from the nest. Their function was to advertise the presence of a nest with a waiting male. A wandering female, attracted by these globules would be courted by the male and encouraged back to the nest.

Unfortunately I did not see this happen, but in an old, out of print book – *Life of the Shore and Shallow Seas* by Dr D.P. Wilson – there is a description of what happens. The female follows the male into the nest, and if all goes well she lays up to 100 eggs. Having performed her function, she swims off into the wide blue yonder. The male, having fertilised the eggs, remains on guard until the young hatch and slowly become able to fend for themselves.

While all this behaviour is fascinating, it is probably more remarkable that such a nest survives long enough to deliver its young into the plankton. After all, the seashore around and below low spring tide can be a fiercely inhospitable environment. Somehow, enough survive tide, surf, wave driven stones and sand, to eventually sustain the population.

Curious epitaphs

On a grave in an Edinburgh churchyard:
Beneath this stone a lump of clay
Lies Uncle Peter Dan'els
Who early in the month of May
Took off his winter flannels.

The calm before the swarm

Mike Silkstone with some amazing facts – and fancies – about the world's most useful insect

Although I've been a country dweller all my 58 years I've never yet seen one. A swarm, that is – but the phenomenon is said to be quite something!

Just imagine. The air alive with a mass of bees circling slowly, like a spiralling magic carpet – the myriad of transparent, furious wings weaving a tissue throbbing with sound, all heading toward the place where the queen has alighted.

Then, just as quickly, each rhythmical wave resolves itself. There is silence as they enfold her, and the shimmering curtain earlier laden with unspeakable menace and anger is transformed into an inoffensive cluster, like a shawl of chenille. This, in bee-keeper parlance, is known as a primary swarm, at whose head the old queen will always be found.

The experienced bee-keeper will wait until the mass has completely gathered together, then shake the bough where they are resting – they will fall into a waiting basket or other receptacle. Where the queen is, the swarm will remain. They will not divide, nor will they sting or grow fierce.

In the days when bees provided the only source of sweetness in our diets, there was much truth in the saying: *'a swarm of bees in May is worth a load of hay.'*

Myths and legends

There are many myths and legends associated with bees and bee-keeping. The ancient Egyptians believed that the tears of the God Re were turned into bees and there is a Breton legend that bees sprang from the tears of the crucified Christ.

At weddings on the island of Guernsey the hives were decorated; in Leicestershire, pieces of bridal cake were placed outside the hives for the bees to enjoy. There was a long-held country custom that bees had to be informed of a death in the family, whereupon black crepe was tied round the hive and the bees would then be prepared to serve their new keeper.

As there are many folktales, so there are various remedies to calm a swarm, should such a thing be necessary. A Somerset recipe was to rub the hive with mint; Yorkshire villagers would dip a branch of flowering elder in water, sprinkle it with sugar and then wave it over the swarm. If all else failed, they would beat a gong in the hope that the noise would have a calming effect!

For the bee-keeper a reasonable crop of honey can be expected every three years, an exceptionally good crop once every 20.

There are many varieties of bees. Yellow honey-bees from the eastern Mediterranean (and even they vary considerably in colour); the Cypriot vicious-in-a-cool-climate bee; the pleasing to handle Italian bee. The black races include British, Dutch and French (with its slender, sharp pointed abdomen, resembling the shape of a wasp). The Caucasian, a native of southern Russia (and said to be docile) and the Carniolan, a native of lower Austria and northern Yugoslavia. Famed for their gentleness, but with a propensity to swarm, they are nevertheless ideal for a novice, and are excellent honey producers, especially if crossed with Italian bees.

Experienced bee-keepers are always prepared to help beginners and there are bee-keepers' associations where novices can learn the craft. Local adult education authorities also often run 'introduction to bee-keeping' courses.

Hierarchy
In the strict hierarchy of the hive, every bee knows its place. The queen's sole duty is to lay eggs, and at the height of the season a good queen may produce 3,000 eggs a day (twice her own body weight). Workers are also female,

Honey bee (Apis mellifera) on meadow clary. Honeys vary enormously, and all have their own characteristics depending on the particular pollens collected.

but sexually under-developed. They build the comb, help rear the brood, clean and guard the hive and collect nectar, pollen and propolis. The drone (the male) is present in the colony in the active season only. Its sole duty is to mate with the queen, and its length of life depends on the will of the workers. Also in the hive will be a number of queen cells.

A cast

After the primary swarm, there is no queen in the hive, but there is much activity, as the workers are thinning the walls of the ripest cell in preparation for the emergence of their new young queen. Only minutes after her birth she has the strength to search the hive for any 'rivals' – other queen cells that may be a threat to her rule. She would destroy these, if not prevented by the workers. (Should two queens be hatched simultaneously, deadly combat begins the moment they emerge from their cradles.) Although there are other queen cells, the occupants are not allowed to emerge, but are kept 'prisoners' and guarded by the workers, who feed them in their cells.

When the young queen is two or three days old, her excitement in the presence of her rivals results in another swarm called a 'cast' – to distinguish it from the primary swarm – and occasionally, in the commotion, one of the imprisoned queens may escape from its cell and join the outgoing bees.

'A swarm of bees in June is worth a silver spoon.'

Honey

In its finished state honey contains sugar and small traces of mineral salts (calcium, phosphorus, magnesium, iron and iodine) and its chief characteristics are the fact that it keeps well and has antiseptic qualities. It has even been used in hospitals to help cure gangrene.

Propolis (a resinous substance collected by bees from the trees) is used in hive construction to fill up cracks, varnish the interior and render the comb cappings impervious to water; it was also used by the ancient Egyptians to mummify the dead. In more recent times, Stradivarius, the great Italian musical instrument maker, used it in the final varnishing of his violins, while in Russia, Lenin's body was preserved using propolis.

Singers suck propolis sweets to ward off throat infection, veterinary surgeons in Minsk use it as an anaesthetic and in England, research is being carried out into the use of propolis in dentistry.

Beeswax as we all know is the basis of all great furniture polishes.

Honeys vary enormously. The first honey of the season will be from fruit blossom and other early flowering plants. Toward the middle of May, the sycamore comes into bloom, and gives a beautifully flavoured, green tinted honey, if the weather is good. There's heather, white clover (my personal favourite) and various others. They all have their own characteristics. Best of all – eat the comb, then you're getting honey, wax, propolis, the lot. ∎

Railway memories

Eric Cresswell unearths a fascinating document

In 1831 a Mr Fergusson travelled from Manchester to Liverpool by rail, a mode of transport then in its infancy. What follows is his account of the journey, originally published in *The Agriculture Quarterly*, and a rare first-hand account of how rail superseded coach travel.

'Having formerly visited the manufactories of Manchester, I proceeded without delay to Liverpool, by the far-famed railway. We started with eight carriages attached to the engine with such imperceptible motion, that it was only when I found myself unable to read a milestone, or to distinguish the features of those who darted past in the opposite direction, that I was led to consult my watch for the rate of travelling; when I found, to my surprise, that the next five miles were done in 15 minutes; nor was it possible, from the precautions so judiciously taken, to feel either anxiety or dread.

'From the powers of the locomotive engines on the railroad, goods and passengers are conveyed from Liverpool to Manchester, a distance of 32 miles, in about two hours. A stage-coach required the whole of the day to perform the journey.

'Among other regulations, a watchman perambulates every half mile to detect any stone or other dangerous impediment upon the rail. As he sees the carriages approaching, if all be right, he stops and extends his arm in sufficient time to enable the engineer to stop the train, should the signal of safety not be displayed.

'As we bowled along, a little circumstance, more ludicrous than dangerous, occasioned a small loss of time. The hook by which No. 2 was attached to No. 1 suddenly gave way, and the engine, with one carriage only, shot off like lightning, leaving the others to follow as they best could. The alarm was, however, quickly given, the engine reversed its movement, while our impetus carried us yet steadily forward, and the whole affair was speedily adjusted.

'The consternation occasioned among the coach-and-horse owners by this wholesale mode of travelling, was of course great, and heavy individual losses necessarily incurred, with much jealousy and ill-will towards the intruder. A knight of the whip, who had been forced to drop his reins, mustered up resolution one morning to take a trip by the railway, and, in spite of a very reasonable stock of indignation, soon felt his asperity giving way under the excitement of such a slapping pace, and, ere he had proceeded far, exclaimed in ecstasy to the engineer, "Come now, my lad, that's it, do boil up a bit of a gallop".' ∎

A lost literary talent

David Evans remembers the poet and essayist James Farrar

In 1946, John Middleton Murry, editor of *The Adelphi* magazine, received some essays and poetry from the mother of a young serviceman killed during the war. This was the first time that an editor had seen the work of James Farrar, and Murry eagerly published it.

Henry Williamson – the distinguished author of *Tarka the Otter* – saw the piece in *The Adelphi* and was so inspired by what he saw that he was put in touch with the young man's mother, Margaret. He learned that James, born at Woodford, Essex on October 5 1923, and schooled at Sutton, was greatly influenced in his writing by Williamson himself. Allowed access to all journals, notebooks and war-time letters, Williamson found himself reading high praise for his own work:

'Once more, having read the *Flax of Dream* with unflagging enthusiasm, I feel the old restlessness upon me... by heavens, its beauty, its perception, its moments of untainted inspiration are beyond the realm of paper and print, and almost of man's mind! I am unquieted by the mental backlash of it. It goes deep into my consciousness, like the dream-music of Frederick Delius. If I in my time can create its equal I can go into the earth serenely.'

Farrar's early pieces include a delightful short story, *Oldest Inhabitant*, which recounts how 93-year-old John Wedgewick cheats the village – and especially the gravedigger – out of a fine funeral. Written soon after war broke out, while Farrar worked on a farm in Cornwall, it bears witness to his fascination with dialect and conversation. *Blackthorn* is another fine example of his talent:

They cannot have her for lover,
The lean brown southerly sprites
Who trade sweet breath for blossom
In star-pale April nights.

Though the cherry,
Our Lady of Splendour,
Exquisitely fallen from grace,
Goes forth in white for her lover
In every woodland place;
And the wind-flirt apple, too eager
For innocence when they came,
Paints the dim skies of daybreak
With her gipsy buds of shame –

They cannot have her for lover,
The ice-white wanton sloe,
For she sells her kisses to winter
Whether they come or no.

As soon as he was old enough Farrar volunteered for the RAF and was called up four months after his 18th birthday. Service life suited his cheerful temperament, fulfilling his sense of duty and his enthusiasm for clean, active living. Training took him to bases throughout England and Wales. At Moreton Valence near Gloucester, he wrote:

'...the stream-bed splits, one fork turns right, widens and becomes the respectable, classic water-setting towards the house: the other goes on, surges down a miniature weir of rocks and bends round to the right.

'Inside the bend, among the trees, is an ancient summerhouse. What gaiety it must have seen in summers of the past! – as I sit down in it I am looking straight up the sheet of water at the house, like the popular picture of the Taj Mahal. A typical retreat of Victorian gentry. But now the thatch is soft and rotted, bored by rats, and mossy inside. Straw and thatch-rubbish lie on the grey earthy floor, birds' nest inside the eaves. The place is derelict, and the seasons are slowly breaking it down.

'On the ground inside lies a dead otter. This is the first I have ever seen, but how could I help knowing every detail of it after reading *Tarka*?'

Countryside descriptions still unashamedly reflected Williamson but, in writing up the experiences of his new life, Farrar was developing his own mature style:

'Plenty of fatigue, yes, but whether you're getting into a kite at midnight or getting your flying kit off just before dawn, when your mouth tastes like wet ashes and birdsong isn't even heard and a cock-crow is just a bore; or going to bed at breakfast-time and having breakfast at tea-time – the whole thing is clean out of the rut, you are living importantly. It's a real life instead of a suburban sham.'

Essays such as *Cloudy Dawn (Station Defence)* exude the real flavour of a nightwatch, and his description of airborne night patrols – he was a navigator – captures the black monotony of an unchanging, star-filled sky. *Sister Service* reflects a young man's confusion at the sudden emancipation of women in war-time.

Letters to his mother and brother David, chart his success in the RAF and provide autobiographical context for his fictional pieces. Still

James Farrar: his plane disappeared over the English channel in 1944.

powerfully descriptive, these began to tackle the horrors of war, even before Farrar experienced them in person:

'First there is only the ghost. Far down in the black water, a ghost of light. It is a pallid thing, like a gleam on the side of some great fish that speeds through the depths. Very gradually it rises and gleams a drowned red, and then becomes brighter. And at last begins to writhe, and is a dreadful orange fan racing across the water with a mist of the same light about it.

'The blazing bomber sinks to embrace it. For a long moment, as if in a final agony, it holds off. But it droops. It begins to fly through a vaporous glow as the propeller-tips touch. Then the strength goes out of it, and four white ribbons sear across the face of the water, and very suddenly there is a great brow of spray flung forward, and a slowing surge, and the other bombers are going on alone while a flame dies into the sea far behind them.'

Poems such as *Airman's Wife* and *After Night Offensive* are the product of a sudden maturity that has inevitably been compared to that of Wilfred Owen. *Last Stand in Corn Valley* is a short story about two deserters, while *Johnny Beyond* considers the uncomfortable reactions of others to an invalid's facial disfigurement.

'We live by Death's negligence', Farrar wrote but, in the early hours of July 26 1944, the Mosquito aircraft he was navigating on a mission to intercept a flying bomb was lost over the English Channel and another of his pieces became autobiographical:

'He was twenty, a youth who swung ideals like sword-blades against the granite of his elders' thought. By its nature, the rock won: but he never gave up. He stood knee-deep in kindly condescension. He began to know that he was the untried, the defective in vision; no more than embryo humanity: a kind of mental leper to whom, however, time held out promise of cure.

'Then on many days in the summer of 1940 he outstepped them all by falling down the long sky in a mass of flame, dying. They had no answer to that.'

Quietly reading *The Imagination to the Wraith*, Williamson found himself being addressed through one of his own characters, but the cruelty of war had reversed the roles:

'This is in its fundamentals yours, the conception and the spirit of it, the deep inspiration, and only the present pigment of fact is mine, your brain being dust and your eyes sightless.'

Williamson put together the small collection of country writings, short stories, poems and sketches that bear witness to Farrar's originality; to a spirit that might well have left an indelible mark on 20th century English literature. ∎

The Unreturning Spring, being the collected works of James Farrar, was edited by Henry Williamson and published in 1950 by Williams & Norgate, and in 1968 by Chatto & Windus.

A history of Happy Families

John Wilmot on card games down the years

Playing cards have a long history. They were used for instruction and amusement among adults and children as far back as the 14th century, when adult card games first arrived in Europe. Packs of cards designed to instruct were without suit signs and they provided information on a wide range of topics, from castles and landmarks to science and general knowledge.

In the 19th century the number of children's card games made purely for entertainment began to increase. These were usually known as Quartets, as they still are on the Continent, though an American version of the 1830s was called Authors. They were among the forerunners of the classic 'juvenile pastime' Happy Families.

Happy Families was commissioned by John Jaques and Son of Kirby Street, Hatton Garden in London – a firm which had been in business since 1795. The game was published and registered at Stationers' Hall in 1861, though it was probably available some ten years earlier. Its original designs have often been attributed to the *Punch* artist John Tenniel, who later provided the illustrations for the *Alice* books.

On Victorian cards the 'heads' of each family had names which highlighted some aspect of their trade – names were also connected to each trade by alliteration. Many of them are still recognisable today, though

Back design for Cotswold Happy Families showing Northleach Church.

Cotswold Happy Families reflect traditional work in the modern countryside.

MRS. WATTLE

The Hurdle Maker's Wife

modern children might be puzzled by Block (barber), and Grits (grocer), as well as by the conical sugarloaf Miss Grits is carrying. The Jaques game soon caught on, provoking a host of Busy, Cheery, Funny, Jolly, Jovial and Merry imitators whose names did not always keep the alliterative link.

One game, National Families, used Victorian stereotypes like Mr Gotakoff the Russian and Mr Macaroni the Italian. Perhaps the more sophisticated or Roald Dahl-spiced taste of contemporary children is reflected in the Horrible Families of 1978, published by a Yorkshire building firm, with suitably gruesome appearances by

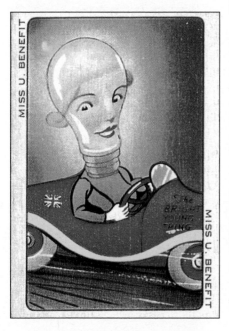

MISS U. BENEFIT

Mr Bind the Mummy and Mr Fang the Vampire.

Many other commercial enterprises have been attracted by the Happy Families card game's promotional possibilities, generating a wealth of ingenious sets for collectors to look out for. These include offerings from the makers of liver salts, lamps (with all the families featured as light-bulbs), cough linctus, lung tonic, biscuits, butter and dogfood, among dozens of others.

As part of a Millennium project,

Miss U. Benefit. Brighter Families (1930) for Cosmos Lamps.

Master Mug the Milkman's Son.

members of the English Playing Card Society have prepared illustrated catalogues of all the so far discovered varieties of Happy Families down the years, as well as other games and playing cards. One of the compilers of these catalogues was Mary Gardiner of Northleach, Gloucestershire. She became interested in the idea of a version of Happy Families reflecting work in the modern countryside. The result was her 1997 Cotswold Happy

MRS. GLAZE

The Stained Glass Maker's Wife

Families in ink and colour wash by the illustrator and photographer Chris Rhodes. The pack was printed in the Gloucestershire village of Bourton-on-the-Water.

All the occupations, such as beekeeper, farrier, forester, gamekeeper, groom, hurdlemaker, stonewaller and so on, can be found within a five-mile radius of Northleach, and some of the pictures are based on real people. A stained glass maker might seem a little exotic, but there are no less than two in Northleach.

Only the ploughman and the shepherd sport traditional dress as a nod to the past, though the shepherd's son is depicted getting his dose of chemicals as he dips a sheep. The others have contemporary clothes, though as Mrs Gardiner says,

A card from the 1997 Cotswold Happy Families collection.

Mrs. Gotakoff the Russian's Wife.

Mrs Gotakoff from the Globe National Families.

'Nowadays everyone seems to go around in jeans'. If the cards for the venerable family game continue to change with the times who knows what the characters may be wearing a hundred years from now?

Sets of Cotswolds Happy Families are available from Mrs Mary Gardiner, Copse View, Northleach, Gloucestershire GL54 3JJ at £3.50 plus 60p post and packing. (Tel: 01451 860606). For the English Playing Card Society send an SAE to Donald Welsh, 11 Pierrepont Street, Bath BA1 1LA. (Tel: 01225 465218.)

Tailcorn

In many ancient houses there is a curious feature built into the staircase. The third or fourth step from the bottom is built an inch or so higher than all the other steps. Those who live in the house quickly get used to this slight difference and never trip up. The unsuspecting burglar creeping into the house at night on the other hand subconsciously registers the height of the first few steps and then stumbles on the higher step. With luck the noise wakes the household and the burglar leaves empty handed or is apprehended.

A treasured collection

Michelle Corps explores the biggest picture library in the world

The Hulton Getty Picture Collection is the biggest photographic archive in the world with an estimated 20 million images. Mark Getty, grandson of oil tycoon John Paul Getty and his business partner, Jonathan Klein bought the collection in 1996, but it all started in 1947 with Edward Hulton, publisher of the popular national weekly news magazine *Picture Post*. When *Picture Post* closed in 1957 its huge collection of superb black and white photographs passed to the BBC.

By 1988 when the collection was again sold, this time to cable television entrepreneur Brian Deutsch, 100 other collections, including Fox Photos had been added to the already enormous archive.

Many images show scenes from our vanished countryside – craftsmen and women, ancient houses and unspoiled land-scapes, but Hulton Getty also boasts work by some of the world's greatest photographers, including 19th century mas-

The Hulton Collection includes a vast number of country images – like this splendid picture of an elderly thatcher at work in 1948.

Above: It's 1920 and Somerset women strip withies (willow branches) by hand for use in basket making. Below: A 1935 shot of a woman spinning wool in Wales for what was described at the time as 'Welsh tweed'.

ters Julia Margaret Cameron (1815-79) whose pictures of Tennyson and Darwin are legendary; Felice Beato – known for his brilliant war photographs; Roger Fenton famous for his portraits of Queen Victoria in the 1850s; and Bert Hardy whose pictures of ordinary people helped democratise photography.

Newspapers, magazine and book publishers have always known about and licensed pictures from the collection, but in an attempt to bring these evocative images to a wider audience Hulton Getty has opened a gallery presenting themed exhibitions of pictures from the collection throughout the year. High quality prints can be bought for private or commercial use. Prices start from £50.

Currently at the gallery (running until March 25), is the All for Love exhibition, which promises, according to a spokesman, 'a fun, witty and moving selection of photographs from the archives'.

The focal point of the exhibition is the romantic image of Melrose Abbey – where the heart of Robert the Bruce is buried.

Other prominent photographs in the exhibition include the famous scene from the film *Casablanca* with Humphrey Bogart and Ingrid Bergman and Bobby Moore kissing the trophy after England's World Cup win in 1966. Worth a visit if you're interested in seeing how photographers portray the idea of

Carding wool in the Shetlands, about 1910. Carding or combing teases out the fibres so they can be spun and made strong enough to be woven or knitted.

Melrose Abbey, where Robert the Bruce's heart is buried.

love; from love of the countryside, to the love of a partner, a pet, or even a football team!

If you'd like to buy a Hulton Getty print telephone 020 7579 5700. The Hulton Getty Picture Gallery (tel 020 7376 4525, Fax 020 7376 4524) is at 3 Jubilee Place, London SW3 3TD. You can also visit their website at:www.hultongetty.com. ∎

Wheelwrights Evan Jelbert (left) and his father in their Cornish workshop in 1953. Evan was the sixth generation of Jelberts to work at the trade.

From the archives . . .

Seventy-three-year-old Mr J. Cornock completes a salmon trap or 'putcher' in Oldbury-on-Severn, Gloucestershire, in preparation for the opening of the season. When our picture was taken in 1936 Mr Cornock claimed to be the oldest salmon fisher on the banks of the Severn. He'd been catching salmon – which have now almost disappeared from the river – since he was six. Copies of this splendid photograph are available from Hulton Getty on 020 7376 4525.

Wild life and tame

Brian Martin with readers' natural history observations and queries

·······································

Over-ambitious snake

Mr D.W. Eddison of Bethersden, Kent, took a remarkable photograph (below) of a 3ft-long grass snake that had apparently drowned while trying to swallow a 9in carp in his pond. Although grass snakes can tackle surprisingly large prey, amphibians such as frogs being its main food, they do occasionally come unstuck. Readers may recall the one that died eating a large toad, reported in our Christmas 1998 issue (pages 79/80).

·······································

Desperate martins

Barry Powderhill writes from Clunbury, Shropshire: On September 19 last year, house-martins congregated outside my bedroom window, prior to migrating to Africa. But they had to suffer torrential rain – over 2in in 24 hours – and instead of perching on nearby telephone and electricity cables they clung to my windows and drain-pipes. It was quite disturbing to see 20 or so birds on the windowsill, peering miserably at me, only a few feet away. Furthermore, when I dashed out to see what was happening I saw hundreds more desperately clinging to the stone walls of my cottage. Have any other readers had a similar experience?

[Yes, this has been recorded before. Martins and swallows are noted for their infrequent cata-strophic appearances when caught on migration by sudden cold or wet spells. As they routinely continue to take their main insect prey on the wing throughout migration, they do not need to fatten up ahead of a long journey to the extent that other birds do. Thus, when inclement conditions overtake them they rapidly weaken and die. Exceptionally, this

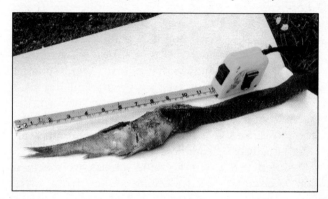

The 3ft-long grass snake that apparently drowned while trying to swallow a 9in carp.

A mole-eating otter. See below.

has happened over a large area of Europe at the same time. Huge mortality of martins and swallows took place during the exceptionally cold first week of October 1974. Trapped by the weather before crossing the Alps, tens of thousands of Hirundines (mostly martins) flew into South East England from Denmark, ahead of fronts moving South West. In Sussex and Kent many exhausted birds actually entered houses as well as roosting on window ledges and trees in an effort to secure warmth and shelter. However, this is usually a fairly local phenomenon so that the species overall does not suffer unduly. It is not unusual for martins to be present in Britain in large numbers in mid-September. Indeed, most pairs have two broods, and with a long incubation/fledging period later birds may not be on the wing until mid-October!]

....

Mole-eating otter

Ray Kennedy of Hexham, Northumberland, took this unusual photo of an otter eating a mole, at the North Pennines Otter Reserve, Bowes Moor, County Durham. Ray reports that the otter devoured the mole with little hesitation, after cap-turing and killing it. Otters are bred at the reserve and the grown young are released into the wild. Generally, otters live almost entirely on fish, crustaceans and aquatic insects, but some take a small proportion of birds and mammals. The feeding pattern reflects the vulnerability and availability of prey species, and would be further restricted by any confinement of the otter. Moles commonly occur in the rich, damp soils surrounding water systems and can even tunnel under river-beds.

....

More itchy foxes

After reading about the magpie and fox in our Oct 29, 1999 issue (page 81), **Geoff Boxall of Orpington, Kent,** sent us a photo (see page 81), which he took from his bedroom window. When foxes were sunning themselves on the roof of the shed next door, a magpie pecked the one lying down. After a while the fox had had enough and they all cleared off.

On the same subject, we received the following note from **Mrs**

Jean Weeks of Lee-on-Solent, Hampshire: 'Last summer a fox came to my garden and appeared to be badly affected by mange on his brush and hindquarters. He made no attempt to run and I believe that it was the same animal I had tamed through feeding in 1998. My resident magpie appeared to do his best to nip the fox's tail, as if in a game, but I believe it was territorial. The National Fox Welfare Society sent me a bottle of homeopathic remedy for mange. As suggested, each morning I put the drops out on a wholemeal honey sandwich, and in the evening I fed him a Marmite sandwich and a handful of small dog biscuits. After about a month of this I was pleased to see the fox improve dramatically. Then I went on holiday for two weeks and when I returned 'Rusty' had gone'.

[Foxes are plagued by parasites and in apparently symbiotic relationships with magpies may allow close approach to effect relief, the birds gaining an easy meal for services rendered. Mange is one of the wide range of diseases and disorders which affect foxes, sometimes so badly they allow close approach by other species. Of course, the sight of a diseased and weakened fox might encourage a magpie to be bolder in asserting territorial rights, actually daring physical attack. However, foxes often have both parasites and diseases at the same time, so we cannot be sure which is the magpie's prime motivator.

....

Crash prevention

Mrs Claire Muller writes from Canada: Those readers who have been troubled by wild birds crashing into their big windows may like to try using the silhouette of a bird of prey. Simply enlarge the drawing (on page 82) to about 20in x 10in and stick it to the glass. Once I did this bird strikes ceased.

[This method has certainly proved a good deterrent and there is no need to be too fussy about the size of the image as birds of prey vary considerably in real life. However, in many

A magpie (just visible to the left of the fox's ear) in stalking mode. See page 80.

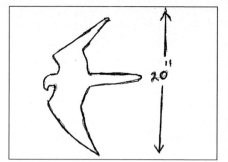

A hawk to keep the birds at bay.
See previous page.

cases it is unlikely to prevent all strikes, especially where the approach view to the window is short.]

••••••••••••••••••••••••••••••••

Daring doves
The item 'Aggressive doves' in our Aug 13, 1999 issue (page 82) prompted a lively postbag. *Michael Gainsford writes from Burbage, Leics:* In our garden collared doves are the most aggressive birds, barring the odd sparrowhawk which relishes dove as a meal. We have seen them attack woodpigeons and jackdaws, but their worst ire seems to be reserved for magpies, and the doves generally come out on top. However, we have never seen them attack smaller birds.

Andrew Wilson writes from Haselor, Warwickshire: The collared doves which feed on our bird table seem tolerant of other birds except jackdaws, often successfully driving them away from the food.

John Alcock writes from Wootton Wawen, Warwickshire: I too have seen collared doves behaving aggressively towards woodpigeons, driving the formerly resident pigeons to the outermost fringes of our surrounding farmland. They also frequently chase off magpies. Once, when several magpies drove a neighbour's cat to take refuge under a car, a collared dove even appeared to join forces to drive the magpies away.

Mr R. Stevens of Roundway, Wiltshire sent us a photograph of a collared dove confronting a magpie in his garden (see below).

[The collared dove appears to have exploited a vacant ecological niche, and since its colonisation in 1952 has spread to most parts of the British Isles, but now it appears to be having an increasingly significant impact on native birdlife.] ■

Magpie meets dove. See above.

If you have any queries or observations write to Brian Martin, c/o The Countryman and please enclose an SAE.

Ramblers' Association news

Jackie Sanders on the problem of blocked footpaths

The Ramblers' Association (RA) has had a great start to the 21st century. On January 14 it won its long-awaited case over the footpath that runs across the East Sussex estate of controversial multi-millionaire Nicholas Van Hoogstraten.

Lewes magistrates court found that the 100-year old path on the High Cross Estate, near Uckfield, was illegally blocked by a barbed-wire fence, a locked gate, refrigeration units and a barn. The company currently registered as the owner of the land, Rarebargain Ltd, was fined £1,600 and ordered to pay costs of £3,500.

Executive committee member Kate Ashbrook, who brought the private action on behalf of the RA, called the ruling 'a victory for the British public'. Unfortunately, despite the magistrate's decision, the path is still blocked, and the RA is now considering further legal action to force the landowner to remove the obstructions.

'It's unsatisfactory that a magistrate can find someone guilty but not order the removal of obstructions,' said Ms Ashbrook. 'We want to get the law changed and will be lobbying the Government. This will be a good example of why the law needs to be strengthened.'

Meanwhile, the RA will continue in its attempts to ensure that the 140,000-mile footpath network in England and Wales is fully open and kept in good order for everyone to enjoy. Sadly, there is still much to be done. New figures from the Audit Commission reveal that a quarter of English and more than half of Welsh paths were obstructed or blocked in 1998/99.

Yet under Target 2000, set up in 1987 by the then Countryside Commission, all local highway authorities were supposed to ensure that every footpath in their area was in usable condition by the year 2000. In fact, only the Isle of Wight claims to have achieved this goal, and we've started the new millennium with thousands of miles of footpaths still blocked.

Over the past year, the RA has been highlighting the appalling state of the footpath network in North Yorkshire. The county was branded as the worst in England for blocked and obstructed footpaths last June, after research by RA volunteers.

That's why the RA has chosen Lightwater Valley Theme Park, near Ripon, as the site of its first footpath rally, planned for Sunday April 9. The action starts at 11.30am, with speeches at midday from RA Vice President Janet Street-Porter, current President Andrew Bennett MP and Kate Ashbrook.

The speeches will be followed by a number of walks. The rally is open to everyone who cares

Mending a broken gate: 'Thousands of miles of English and Welsh footpaths are still blocked or obstructed'.

Ramblers' Association

about the state of our country's footpaths. More information can be found on our website at www.ramblers.org.uk, or by phoning RA footpaths campaigner Jacquetta Fewster on 020 7339 8535.

Freedom to roam

Something else to look forward to in the near future is, of course, the introduction of a legal freedom to roam. This will come into law as part of the Government's Countryside Bill. Once introduced, the public will be given access to mountains, moors, heath, down and common land in England and Wales.

This is surely great news for all those who love the countryside. And yet not everyone has been so positive. Since the Government announced its plans for a freedom to roam bill last November, the public has been inundated with misinformation and scaremongering from some sections of the landowning lobby. In fact, some critics have gone so far as to call the freedom to roam a 'trespassers' charter' and have said that it will lead to a loss of privacy.

This is, of course, untrue. The freedom to roam is not a licence to trespass. Private land will remain exactly that, and we will all continue to enjoy privacy in our own homes. All the new law will do is allow people to walk on specific, mapped areas of open, uncultivated land, subject to common-sense restrictions to protect agriculture, wildlife and the environment.

Of course, it's not only countryside users who will benefit from the freedom to roam. Recent research in Wales found that greater access to the countryside will play a key role in attracting more visitors to the country. More visitors mean more money, and a much-needed boost to the rural economy.

Although it is unclear how long the Countryside Bill will take to pass through Parliament, the Government has promised that a legal freedom to roam will be in place within two years. Some RA members got an opportunity to thank Deputy Prime Minister John Prescott in person for this promise, when he accompanied them on a three-mile walk in the Yorkshire Dales in January. The ramblers made the most of the occasion by also presenting Mr Prescott with almost 500 thank you letters, in appreciation of his call for the South Downs and New Forest to be given National Park status.

The Deputy PM's announcement on the proposed Parks, made last September, has certainly been well received by the public. An NOP opinion poll, commissioned by the Ramblers in December, found that four out of five people back the decision. Support was equally high from those who live and work in the two areas, sending a clear signal to those local authorities which have so far opposed the proposals.

A victory in court, discussions on two new National Parks and the prospect of the freedom to roam – and it's barely springtime! What a great century this is shaping up to be for the RA and countryside lovers everywhere. ∎

Dear newsagent, please reserve me a copy of
***The Countryman* every six weeks**

Name _____

Address _____

_____

_____

Telephone _____

Curiouser and curiouser

John Vince with more readers' mysteries and queries

In this issue we identify a mystery keyhole and find out more about the days when horses were more numerous than cars.

A dough trough from eastern Europe is discovered in a Sussex barn. From Canada and parts of the UK the details of a curious saw (Dec 10, 1999) are revealed. Questions about post boxes emerge from Gloucestershire and we have found an old notice which reminds us of the social structure of Victorian England.

A recycled sundial
Andrew Wilson from Alcester, in Warwickshire, writes to tell us that the sundial converted into a keyhole (Oct 29, 1999) is to be seen on the church door at Sydenham, Oxon.

A wheelwright discovered
H.M. Jones, now of Shoreham, Sussex, was brought up on a farm in Oxfordshire and he recognised our Tompkins wagon (p93, Oct 29, 1999). On the wagon's near side the name of the builder 'Sharp, Wheelwright, Arncott' is recorded.

He knew the builder, Will Sharp, and often watched him making wheels. The wheelwright's son, George, was in the same class as Mr Jones and did the lettering on the vehicles his father made. Will Sharp's wagon can now be seen at the Cogges Manor Farm Museum, Witney, Oxfordshire.

Horsedrawn days
Our earlier mention of lamplighters has prompted Mrs E. Fox, who used to live in Birmingham, to tell us about the tradesmen she recalls when deliveries were made by horse and cart. She remembers the call of the muffin man who came with his pony cart, and the milkman who measured out the milk with his measure from a large churn. The same milk float was also used to deliver 'grain' – used brewers' hops – to the back gardens where it was employed as a fertiliser. Coal also arrived by cart and cost 1s 6d a hundredweight! Perhaps other readers can tell us about the tradition of home deliveries which supermarkets seem to have suddenly rediscovered.

Mixing the dough
Peter Hill from Hove, Sussex, sends us a photograph (Fig 1) of a solid-

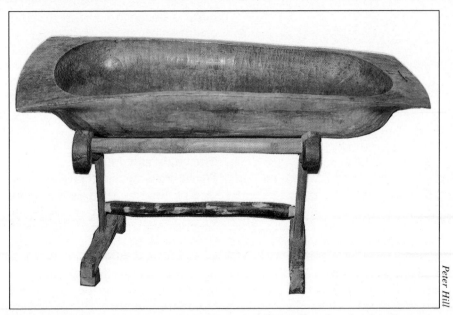

Fig 1: Dough trough from eastern Europe – it is basically a log that has been hollowed out.

wood dough trough which came from eastern Europe, possibly Hungary. The trough is almost 5ft long, 1ft 8in wide and about 8in deep. It is made of a softwood, possibly sycamore, and the marks of the gouge used to hollow out the interior can be clearly seen. This fine example of treenware has its own stand and as the photograph shows this is also fashioned in a rural manner. The stretcher which links the two legs still retains some of its bark.

Together these two examples of craftsmanship represent a tradition which has almost, but not quite, disappeared. Confronted by such a large trough you wonder just

how long it took to hollow out the middle. Such a task demanded

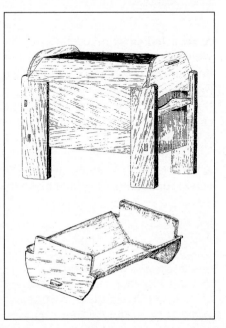

Fig 2: 15th century ark with a lid upside down ready for dough making.

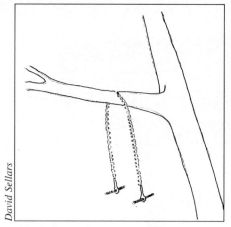

David Sellars

Fig 3: How the chain saw kit was used.

considerable skill. As the bowl became deeper, great care had to be exercised so that the bottom remained intact and unbroken! This unusual example can be seen at the museum at West Blatchington Windmill, Hove, Sussex (open from Easter to September – details on 01273 776017.)

In England dough troughs were constructed from planks, from the 18th century onwards, and had a flat lid which was closed so that the dough could rise.

An older style of dough trough can be seen at Mary Arden's House, Wilmcote, Warwickshire. This takes the form of an 'ark' (Fig 2) which has plank sides and a lid which can be turned upside down to

Fig 4: In the Post Office at Wendover in Buckinghamshire, there is a replica Penfold box, made by a retired postman. It is embellished with an 1850 style Post Office notice which we illustrate here. Do any other period notices like this one survive? Where is the oldest post box to be found?

make a dough trough. In the 15th century when most houses of substance had furniture of this kind, the bread was stored in it and the lid kept flies away. There is another example at Montacute House in Somerset (National Trust).

••••••••••••••••••••••••••••••••••••

The chain saw kit
We have had a large postbag concerning the saw kit (Dec 10, 1999) belonging to Mr C.N. Jackson. Several readers report that such saws could be bought from army surplus stores after World War II – for as much as 3s 6d! Many of these saw kits bore the traditional Ordnance mark (the upward pointing arrow head). Older examples are also known. One kit is dated 1915 but another seems to be even earlier.

The weight of evidence indicates that this ingenious saw had a military use. It was capable of speedily clearing tree branches which were likely to obstruct artillery. A saw of this type could be used by one soldier. We are grateful

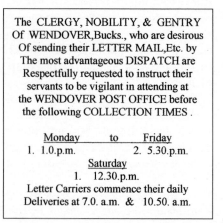

The CLERGY, NOBILITY, & GENTRY
Of WENDOVER,Bucks., who are desirous
Of sending their LETTER MAIL,Etc. by
The most advantageous DISPATCH are
Respectfully requested to instruct their
servants to be vigilant in attending at
the WENDOVER POST OFFICE before
the following COLLECTION TIMES .

Monday	to	Friday
1. 1.0.p.m.		2. 5.30.p.m.

Saturday
1. 12.30.p.m.
Letter Carriers commence their daily
Deliveries at 7.0. a.m. & 10.50. a.m.

to David Sellars, from Thurso, for providing the drawing (Fig 3) which shows how the saw was deployed. Mr L.C. Peploe's very old saw kit has been donated to the fascinating Trevarno Gardens Museum at Helston in Cornwall (more information on 01326 574274).

It would be a mistake to think that these very useful tools are things of the past. David Humphrey from British Columbia, Canada sends us details of a chain saw kit still on sale there, priced $29.95. As the catalogue says this saw 'weighs less than a pound, needs no fuel and slices through hardwood like butter!'. Mrs Claire Wailer, of Ontario, also reported the usefulness of this type of saw in her part of the world. ■

Fig 5: A 'Penfold post box' seen in Cheltenham by a reader.
This early example has a downward slope inside the letter slot. This was found to allow the rain to run inside. To prevent the letters getting wet an enamel plate was later fixed to the top edge of the slot. As this has served for more than a century we may guess that the addition was effective. Do any readers know of other ancient boxes which are still in place and in use? Notice the monogram VR – Victoria Regina.

We appreciate all the letters we have received and are sorry that space prevents us acknowledging you individually. Please keep writing.

One countryman to another

Readers' stories, and memories of life earlier this century

∙∙∙∙∙∙∙∙∙∙∙∙∙∙∙∙∙∙∙∙∙∙∙∙∙∙∙∙∙∙∙∙∙∙∙∙

When the customer was always right

J. Dorothy Cleal on working in a grocery shop for 7s 6d a week

Careers advice didn't loom large in the curriculum of pre-war elementary schools. I never remember the subject cropping up, although, as I passed my 14th birthday, the matter began to nag at me. In my previous school, a village establishment in an almost feudal community, girls who had been considered either too dumb or too poor to be considered for the grammar school were assumed to be fodder for the domestic service market.

Towards the end of term, the local ladies would descend like vultures to make their requirements known to the headmaster – or, in the case of the real aristocracy, feed those requirements into a sort of grapevine – and names would be suggested and interviews arranged. I had made up my mind quite early that domestic service wasn't my scene – though I flirted with the idea fleetingly at the age of about ten, when I thought that being a parlour-maid might be a stepping stone to realising my ambition of marrying into the nobility.

But when my family left the village and moved into a small town nearby, I found that shops had taken over from 'service' as the obvious choice for school-leavers of my level, and that was fine with me.

The manager of a local grocery shop came to the school and asked the headmistress if she had any girls available for work; I was 14, and eligible. The job on offer was that of cashier, and after an interview which consisted of nothing more than showing him that I could write my name and address clearly and add up a column of figures, I was engaged to start at once. My mother, who was with me, hesitated when he mentioned the wage: 7s 6d a week, (which seemed riches to me) for a week which proved to average 45 hours, once nearer 50.

The longest days were Friday and Saturday, the days when the weekly bills were paid and most people did their main shopping. The shop closed at 7pm on Fridays and 8pm on Saturdays, and people would be shopping right up to the last moment. After which I had to try and make the cash balance, which it never did – never, I think, even once.

A school photograph of Dorothy Cleal aged 14, just before she went to work in the grocer's shop.

The pressure was unnerving on those days too, for the assistants would get irritable if the little tin cups took too long to get back to the counters with their change, and they would rattle the wires, so while I fumed and fretted to get done, the accompanying jangling of wires was joined by the jangling of my fragile nerves. I really hated Fridays and Saturdays, especially as I knew my non-shop-working friends were out to play or going to the pictures.

The shop I worked in was a branch of a very small chain of grocery stores based in Surrey; I think there were only three branches. The branch in our Hertfordshire town – hardly more than a village in those days – was in a very old building which had once been an inn.

It smelled delicious, as old-fashioned grocers always did. There was a provisions counter on the right as you entered, with a marble top and great mounds of butter which were slapped and patted between wooden boards, then weighed and wrapped. And there were massive hams, and the cheeses were cut with a wire to suit your exact requirements, and you could sample a sliver before you made your choice. On the opposite counter were groceries, and that included all the spices of Araby, and teas from various parts of the Orient, and different kinds of loose coffee. (The less important customers were catered for by the provision of Camp, in bottles, but these were tucked away, for they were thought to lower the tone, and such customers were served with thinly veiled disdain).

In the darker recesses of the shop were wines and spirits, dispensed by the shop manager himself, with much bowing and scraping if the social position of the customer appeared to merit it. I heartily loathed the shop manager, and the feeling appeared to be mutual, for he could never resist getting little digs at me.

I actually felt quite ill in his presence. He had a noiseless, rushing sort of walk, and a rapid way of talking with which his dentures never quite caught up. I got the impression that he thought me too big for my boots, and can only account for this by the fact that I didn't speak with the local accent as my colleagues did. Whatever the reason, he never missed an opportunity to 'take me down a peg'. He really was quite cruel. He was sarcastic, pausing after what he considered to be a crushing little witticism to meet the eyes of other members of the staff, who dutifully smirked.

I had first encountered him when my family moved into the town, a few months earlier. My mother had given me a penny and asked me to go to the shop in the school dinner break to buy a block of salt. I said: 'What if it's tuppence?' 'It won't be,' she said firmly. But it was indeed tuppence, and it was this man who had served me, when I had to confess that I only had a penny – and this in front of my new school friends, and in a nearly empty shop, so that every assistant witnessed my shame. Later, I learned from my mother that she had only had a penny in her purse that day. I vowed that I would never go into that shop again, and in the event could only do so by convincing myself that I was too insignificant for anyone to remember me. But the odious Mr T remembered, you may depend, and he never let me forget that he remembered.

The store had a drapery department, entered separately, with two long counters, and bales of wonderful-smelling materials, and dressmakers' busts of Edwardian proportions draped with lace collars and georgette scarves. At the rear, up some steps and under an arch, there was a section where corsets and underwear and even more delicate items could be purchased; some of the corsets looked as though they had been there since the death of Queen Alexandra, and probably had, for they had a musty, moth-bally smell, and I never saw anyone buying them.

The department was presided over by an old-young woman, probably no more than 24 or 25, but middle aged in her gait and demeanour, with her hair in neat brown marcel waves, and dressed demurely in navy blue. She was assisted by a giggly 16-year-old whom she was trying (without much success) to train in the niceties of her calling.

In all departments there were of course the high, round chairs almost always found in shops then. And customers were treated almost reverently; always called 'Madam' (few 'Sirs' crossed the threshold). This might be omitted if the customer was personally known to the assistant, in which case she was addressed by name, and even then, the tone used was quite different from that used when they met elsewhere. Above the counters were the wooden or metal cups into which the money and ticket were placed when the purchase was completed; a handle was then pulled and the cup would go whirring across the shop and disappear through a hole high in the wall, ending up in what was really rather like a little ski-lift terminus, above a high, old-fashioned desk, such as is sometimes seen in Dickens illustrations. This was my domain.

When I think of the frugal staffing in the big modern supermarkets, I marvel at the number of employees it took to run a small-town grocers in those pre-war days. In addition to a counter staff of about seven, there were two or three men in the stock room besides the shop manager, and three girls in the office including myself, plus the general manager, who rarely appeared before the public.

Two of the stockroom men were also van drivers, who delivered orders to outlying villages, orders which had been collected earlier in the week by two older men who rode out on bicycles. Then there was a gangling youth of about my own age who delivered in the town, on his tradesman's bike. He, poor lad, imagined himself to be in love with me, and would find excuses to come into the office and stand by my desk gazing wordlessly, to my cringing embarrassment and the general hilarity of the rest of the staff. When he started lying in wait for me when I finished work (always later than anyone else) I felt it was time to be cruel to be kind, and eventually he got the message. Anxious though I was to be the object of some man's undying love, I felt that at 14 I was a bit young to settle for the likes of poor Cyril.

The war came. I gave up my job – by mutual agreement, I suspect – in the last week of that hot, unreal week of peace. I had long been considered 'delicate', and my health was giving cause for concern. In the days leading up to that dramatic weekend, the younger men on the staff had already received their 'papers', for they were in the Territorials, and suddenly they were being very serious, and everyone was being nice to them. There were gloomy recollections of 'the last lot', and even the shop manager forgot to be horrid in the general anxiety.

The old order was dying. Before long, rationing and shortages would mean that it was the customer who had to turn on the wheedling charm. And soon the shelves would empty and national service would make shop assistants a declining breed, no longer at the mercy of exacting customers. It was a time, perhaps, for the settling of old scores – and the end of an era.

....

The Black Gate
Hugh Barrett on how features in the countryside survive in the language of children

Our farm was in a small rural Suffolk village. In 1950 the village primary – the only school – had two teachers, and around 25 pupils of whom at the time two were ours. A large tortoise stove glowed red hot in winter, and the earth closet buckets in a little brick shed at the back were emptied over the fence into little holes dug in my adjacent field. The teaching was such that no child ever left unable to read, write and do simple sums.

There were two sources of knowledge; in the classroom, and in the playground. One day I met our eight-year-old son as he trotted into the farmyard. I asked him what he had been doing. 'We've been playing up at the Black Gate' he replied. Not ever having heard of the Black Gate I asked where it was. 'It's where you go into Mr Kindred's sugar-beet field' he replied.

Having farmed there for years, I

thought I knew every field and every gate within a mile or more, and of the few gates there were, none was black. And the sugar-beet field my son spoke of certainly had no gate at all. I asked him why this place was called the Black Gate. His reply failed to enlighten me much. 'Oh, that's what we (meaning his school friends) always call it.'

Over a period of a few weeks I asked other boys if they knew where the Black Gate was; all of them knew exactly, but none had any idea why it was so called.

I became intrigued with this and asked among older, and not so old people round the village if they had an answer to the puzzle. For a long time I got nothing but 'don't know', 'don't never recollect that, can't help you there'. Several told me there never had been a gate at that spot. Then one day I happened on a very old man who, although no longer living in the village, had worked there for most of his life. With him, bit by bit, for he was a tease, I struck gold.

'Ah guv'nor, the gate were red!'

I said it was odd then that it should be called black.

'So you might think, but I can tell you the last gate into that field were an old red thing made out of bits of a broken threshing machine. There were just a few broken rails from it lying around in the ditch when I worked there'. He paused. 'Now to tell you the truth, I never did see no Black Gate, but the men I worked with always spoke as if it still hung there. And that's right, there had been a gate painted black at one time in the past. No doubt about it.'

But when? 'They were old men then, 60, 70 year old: I'm 84, so I reckon that gate must have rotted and disappeared in the middle of last century!'

How then, in such a small village did knowledge of a physical feature that had vanished perhaps 150 years earlier, (and been wiped from the memories of the adult population) – how did it live through generations of children and still be current among nine and ten year olds?

Perhaps the learned profession has the answer. What mechanisms are involved? I remain curious. Sadly, the village school closed years ago and today's children who would have been a source for research into this oddly selective folk memory now live in a world where field gates of any colour have no meaning and no place in their lives. ■

Country diary

Humphrey Phelps on gumboots and nightmare regulations

An elegant moon shone brightly through the mist to greet the first morning of the new year. The following days were dark and damp and dismal, yet each morning birds sang as though spring had already arrived. Aconites, snowdrops and periwinkles flowered, catkins swung daintily in a breeze and moles became very active. After weeks of rain the fields are sodden; as I walk across them my gumboots make a depressing squelch. I heard somewhere that computers have been the greatest invention or boon for agriculture during the last hundred years – I rather think that gumboots have a far better claim to that distinction.

Our milk production was low during December and early January, then three or four more cows calved and we got on to some better quality silage and production increased by 25 per cent. The lesson is obvious, make better quality silage. But so much depends on the weather in order to make good hay and silage. Machinery has helped farmers to beat the weather but despite that and all the wonders of science, weather is still the master. Perhaps it's right that it should be so; man has already become a danger to mankind, all life in fact, because of his arrogance. But, as a neighbour once said, 'Farming keeps a man humble'. Well, yes, up to a point but I confess I don't always see humility in some farmers.

And still they come; more regulations and restrictions, more and more forms. All press hard upon the working farmer who has far better things to do than sit at a desk for hours, and days on end pandering to the whims and fads of bureaucrats with nothing better to do. Fifty years ago, Henry Warren, author of several country books, saw the shape of things to come. Small farmers, small traders and craftsmen would, he said, be hedged round with restrictions and smothered in forms. Their lives would be made a hell and the spirit scared out of them. Small farms would be merged with big ones and turned into factories. The country made into something like the towns. Now it's all coming to pass or has already done so. Hardly a month goes by without hearing of another real farmer giving up in despair. Decent countrymen who have never done anyone any harm but have been driven out by falling returns and an avalanche of regulations, restrictions, inspections and forms.

I see small farms merged into larger holdings, turned into 'equestrian centres' or golf courses. Farmhouses sold off, barns turned into houses or flats. The country may not be like the town yet, but it's getting awfully like suburbia. Shops, pubs and other services have closed, and now more village post offices are under threat of closure in the name of modernisation.

By mistake, government figures showing the drastic decline in farming incomes have been disclosed and agriculture is in a severe crisis, but despite aid being available, the government prefers to issue vacuous slogans. All that most farmers want is fair play but real farmers lack an effective organisation or voice. Many of them still cling to the NFU which must be a triumph of hope over experience. As the late Alan Clark said, 'More and more of the people who call the shots on the NFU are the nasty, computer-driven 'barons' who drench everything with nitrates and rip off the CAP'.

A few months ago we were subjected to a lengthy questionnaire and our premises inspected by a Milk Marque representative and a few weeks later another lengthy questionnaire by MAFF. Next week a Ministry vet is coming to test all our cattle. On Thursday the County Council is getting in on the act by sending someone to examine our movement of animals book, our animal medicine book, the register of births, the ear tags in stock and who knows what else. On the second day of the test the Ministry vet will also examine the movement and medicine books. And Milk Marque takes regular milk samples to test for butterfat, protein, hygiene, antibiotics and water. As yet we don't know who or what will be coming or what about, next week, next month.

A couple of years ago all new-born calves had to have plastic tags in their left ears in addition to the usual metal ones in their right ears. In some ways the plastic ones are an improvement as the numbers are more easily seen. Unfortunately these bigger tags are more likely to get caught in something and torn out. Last year the Ministry decided all calves born on or after January 1 should have a different system of numbering. But the Ministry couldn't decide what those numbers should be, so farmers couldn't order the new tags from the manfacturers. At last the Ministry realised this and extended the period for the old system. Naturally enough with this new system coming into force, farmers didn't order a large number of old tags. January 1 has come and gone, calves have been born, the old tags almost used up and

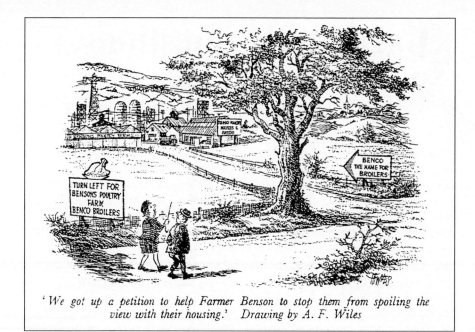

'We got up a petition to help Farmer Benson to stop them from spoiling the view with their housing.' Drawing by A. F. Wiles

A cartoon by A.F. Wiles, from a book by Henry Warren, points to the increasing industrialisation of farming – in the 1940s!

the manufacturers, inundated with orders, haven't been able to supply new tags at such short notice owing to the Ministry's indecision and delay. But calves have to be ear-tagged within 36 hours of birth and their passport applications complete with eartag numbers received by MAFF within seven days of tagging. If MAFF do not receive the applications within that time the calves must be destroyed. And when the passports come from MAFF more often than not there are mistakes which the farmer has to correct and then return the passports to MAFF. One way and another it's a fair old game. Is it a case of those whom MAFF wish to destroy, it first sends mad? However, in fairness, I must say that almost without exception we've had nothing but courtesy and help from the Ministry vets and officials with whom we've been in contact. The confusion etc, is not their fault and I dare say it's all enough to drive them mad too.

The moon is shining brightly and the stars are twinkling, a fine, clear night with a nip of frost in the air, when I go out late to look at some freshly calved cows. All is silent apart from the low murmur of a cow and the occasional hoot of an owl. By the light of my lamp the cows and calves, well bedded-down with bright straw, are a heart warming sight. And, creaturely kind, one cow started to lick her calf. As I stood and stared and took my fill of this, all the tribulations of farming today were cast aside – momentarily at least. ∎

Gardeners' questions...

Answered by Val Bourne

Inedible apricots

Mr J. Halliday writes from Maidstone in Kent: About eight years ago my daughter gave me an apricot tree about 15in high in a sizable tub, which flowered and then gave me some rather dry and not very edible apricots. Two years ago it was flagging and we moved it to a sheltered spot in the back garden. It responded and grew about six, 5ft long shoots with lance-head shaped leaves. But there are no flowers and no fruit, although the leaves fall in the autumn and reappear in the spring.

It's no great loss, but an intriguing event for a small, innocent looking plant. Can you throw some light on it please? Apricots are a subject close to my heart.

[My partner has an apricot tree against the south-west facing wall of his garden and if there's a bumper harvest – which happens every three or four years – we feast on apricots. There was 43lb of fruit one summer, but the blossom was gently hand pollinated with an artist's brush. In theory, given a warm sheltered sunny site, your tree should produce fruit every year. But late frosts, cold springs and the tree's general vigour mean that, in my experience, the apricot crop will vary. Apricots are usually grafted on to a vigorous root stock and you need to establish whether or not your tree is grafted by looking for a knobbly area about*

Apricots are suited to a warm sheltered sunny site.

6in above the ground. If the new long shoots are above the graft – all well and good. Leave them alone. If the new growth is coming from the root-stock, you need to ruthlessly cut it out and force the tree to produce some new shoots above the graft. Apricots flower on the side shoots, which are best cut back to six or eight leaves. To improve the chance of flowering further, feed your apricot tree now with a heavy dose of sulphur of potash – 4oz per square yard – which promotes flowers. Then feed twice a year (in March and September) with a lighter dose – 2oz per square yard. If readers are thinking of planting an apricot, choose 'Moorpark', a firm, orange apricot which ripens in August – it's the most reliable in England. Good luck and I hope that you manage to get some fruit this summer.]

Gooseberry blight

Mr and Mrs Wilson write from Kendal in Cumbria: In spite of spraying for American blight on gooseberries, we've had to dig out and destroy our bushes. Although we've replaced them with a blight-resistant variety, after two years our bushes got the blight again. The plants will have to be replaced or the growing of gooseberries abandoned. It would be helpful to know where the blight comes from – is it in the ground or the air? Or could it be that it drops from the high overhanging branches of an 80ft high lime tree? Could you also recommend a really efficient spray?

[American gooseberry blight is a form of mildew which coats the stems, the leaves and the fruits with a white powder. It's an air-borne disease, which means that bushes need to be well spaced and effectively pruned to help the air to circulate. Any diseased wood needs burning and any leaves or fruit which drop also need destroying. Mildew is often caused by drought stress and although the Lake District is one of the wettest areas in the country, your gooseberries may well be short of water.

Gooseberry roots are very shallow, so they need a cool, fertile soil. Although they are very tolerant of shade, and crop heavily in a small area – which makes them ideal plants for small gardens – they would be very stressed in soil which has been dried out by a tall lime tree. I would strongly suggest a new position for your gooseberry bushes, rather than scrapping them. Replant them, after a strong cut back, well away from the tree.

Don't feed your gooseberries with a nitrogen rich fertiliser, it will produce soft sappy growth which is far more likely to get mildew. I wouldn't recommend a manufactured spray, because you have to eat gooseberries after a short growing season and it's inevitable that you will end up ingesting some of the chemicals. Instead use a mixture of half a pound of soft soap, one pound of washing soda and five gallons of water – spraying it on in mid-summer and then again in early spring, and when the fruit has set. But I honestly think if you move the plants into soil which isn't dried out by tree roots, the problem will cure itself.]

Eternal weed

Trevor Hambly writes from Seaview on the Isle of Wight: Your advice on the enclosed weed would be much appreciated. It has spread from the garden wall and invaded the lawn, completely covering some areas. Sodium chlorate has killed it off on the walls, as has Weedol – but Verdone isn't any good. Is there a selective weed-killer or another approach?

[Trevor has kindly sent me a specimen inside a plastic bag but it's too dried to identify with certainty. It has certainly got creeping stems, which leads to me to believe it's a perennial weed (one which reappears every year). Sodium chlorate kills everything in its wake and it's usually only used on paths and drives. Weedol kills the green growth, but not the root, and is only effective on annual weeds – like bitter cress. So I'm puzzled by the fact that Weedol has worked on this one. There isn't a specific or magic solution to eradicate any weed and once creeping weeds get into lawns they are very difficult, because every time you mow you chop it up and it sprouts back into the lawn. The best solution is to use a wire rake and tweak as much out as you can, and over-sow the lawn with some fresh lawn seed to stop the weeds penetrating bare soil and make it harder to get a grip. If Verdone hasn't worked in the past it's unlikely that other specific weed-killers will, because this creeping weed has a very small leaf and these sprays work on leaves with a much larger surface area than a blade of grass.

Keep removing it and disturbing the root system continually and it will give up – with time.]

Wilting lobster

Rupert Wilson from Enniskillen in County Fermanagh, Northern Ireland writes: I am growing the lobster claw plant (*Clianthus puniceus*) from seed and some of the smaller plants are collapsing at the head. The plant tray is in sufficient heat and getting sufficient water. Also I have successfully grown some of these magnificent plants outside and some have become very large, but this past year they turned white and wilted for no apparent reason. The soil was well drained and they were planted on a south facing wall. These plants did not recover, yet on other occasions plants grew without any trouble. Can you help?

[How I envy you Rupert, because most of us would have to grow this delicate, showy plant in a conservatory. It has divided green leaves and bunches of bright red claw-shaped flowers. It's a New Zealand plant from the warm North Island and Maori people always used to grow it round their doorways, considering it sacred. For that reason, it is seldom found in the wild anymore. It was collected by Joseph Banks in 1769, who found it adorning Maori houses, when accompanying Captain Cook on The Endeavour. Your seedlings have almost certainly damped off with a combination of damp air caused by warm, wet conditions. Tender plants love hot dry air – a rare commodity in Britain during winter. The advice for keep-

ing tender plants through winter is to keep them bone dry and then restart them into life during March or April by watering them well and keeping the greenhouse well ventilated. I would recommend beginning to sow your seed immediately you collect it. The plants outside have almost certainly had a surfeit of warm damp air too. It might be best to try growing one plant in a terracotta container in gritty compost – thereby making sure that the root ball stays well-drained throughout the year. This plant could then be moved to allow the air to circulate round it and put in a dry position. I think the varying weather during subsequent summers has made the difference between some plants thriving some years and others dying. We've had a succession of very dry summers and now they seem to be getting damper again.]

Foolproof foods

Zoe Reynolds writes from Leamington Spa in Warwickshire: I would like to start growing some vegetables but I don't know which are easiest?

[*Most people have small gardens and it's best to choose plants that crop heavily in a small area. It also makes economic sense to grow expensive plants or plants that are difficult to buy in supermarkets. Mangetout peas are one of the easiest plants to grow and you can train them round a tripod of canes. They produce lots of pods, which need picking almost daily and will give you lots of vegetables over several weeks. They crop earlier than peas and are very easy to grow. I would also grow a tripod of French beans, which would crop soon after, and some runner beans – which would grow until the first frosts. Buy some tomato plants in May and plant those in containers, but they will need watering every day. Grow herbs from seed in early May – basil, parsley and chives – and mint and sage plants from a nursery and you'll find that you will always have herbs in summer. Sow some leafy red lettuces – the ones you pick leaves from rather than the hearting ones. If you've still got room, buy two courgette plants. My very favourite garden vegetable, though, is the potato. Try to find room for a few 'earlies' – rocket is an excellent potato which is ready 10 weeks after sowing.]

Jobs for spring

March and April are one of the most testing times of the year for the gardener, because you have to go with your instincts. Every spring is different. In recent years I've known the daffodils flag in 70 degree heat, and winter go straight into summer. Other years, the garden has been pegged back by cold, dry weather until early May. So this is the time of year to develop your skills as a weather prophet. Don't tune into the weather forecast – get out there and take a look. If the soil feels warm and crumbly and there's a sweet smell in the air, then go ahead and plant. If it lies cold and wet and makes you shudder – wait. Catching the weather just right is the whole secret of gardening. Whatever happens in March, we're almost certainly in for a spell of cold dry weather in April, when the 'blackthorn winter strikes', so concentrate your efforts on tidying up, cultivating the soil and eradicating the weeds.

Cultivate your seed bed
If you grow vegetables, you'll almost certainly need a well cultivated seed bed, where you'll plant cabbages and leeks which will need to be planted out in late spring. There's a stage in the year when you can almost hear plants growing – they change by the day. It's because the soil's warmed up. Look for the signs and sow your leek and cabbages then, protecting them against hungry birds with some netting. I'll be serenaded by a chorus of toads all advertising for a mate, but it'll get me up before six in the morning and if the weather's clement I'll be out there.

Early sowings
Easter's late this year, so plant some potatoes in mid March. For once, European law works in our favour and lots of garden centres are selling seed potatoes in kilos (rather than 7lb packs) which makes it easier to grow one or two varieties. Parsnips take a long time to germinate (up to 30 days) and I like to sow a row early in the year. If they fail it gives me time to sow another lot! Broad beans and onion sets also need planting and I'll be planting some parsley seeds too. Warming the soil by pouring on a kettle of warm water – BEFORE SOWING! – does seem to work for parsley.

One year's seed...
A good gardener always picks out a weed when it's in flower. They know that one year's seed means seven years weeds. Actually the reality is even worse, because many weed seeds have 20 years' viability. Getting on top of the weeds now will save you endless time later. The biggest rogues in March and April are the dandelions – exterminate them by digging them out with an old knife or a special long trowel.

Flowers galore
This is the best time to sow sweet peas for most gardeners. Use long deep pots and once they're 3-4in high harden them off outside for a week or so. Then transplant them quickly into well-prepared soil enriched with manure or compost. Place the twiggy sticks around them as you plant. Also sow hardy annuals – pot marigolds, cornflowers, godetias, ladybird and other poppies, nigella and clary directly into the soil. Cover with netting and water well – keeping them watered. The trick is to water them at midday on warmer days – replicating April showers. Also sow sage, chives and other hardy herbs. But only if the soil is warm. Hardy annuals are great garden plants – colourful in July and August and capable (if deadheaded) of keeping going for months. ■

If you have a gardening query write to: Val Bourne, Gardener's questions, The Countryman, 6th floor, King's Reach Tower, Stamford Street, London SE1 9LS.

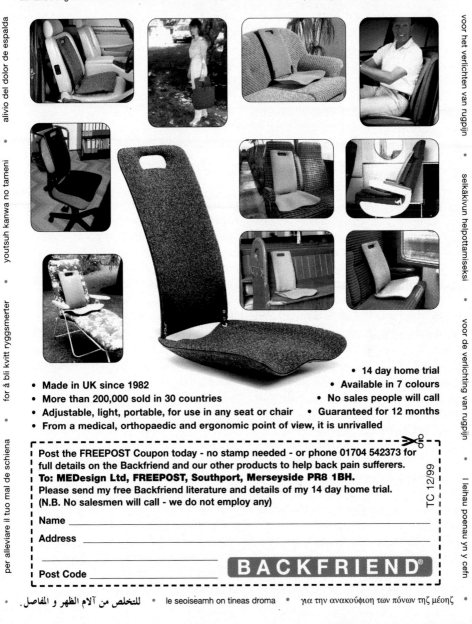

Bookshelf

Records of the past

Tom Quinn looks at new guides to Celtic customs, ancient farming and the old East End

Brian Day's **Chronicles of Celtic Folk Customs** (Hamlyn, £17.99) is a month by month guide to festivals and traditional ceremonies from as far afield as Brittany, Wales, the Isle of Man, Cornwall and Scotland. The book is comprehensive, well illustrated (with many archive photos) and detailed.

Here you will find, for example, the Ne'er Day Ba' Ball in Kirkwall Orkney, a vast football match that involves virtually every male inhabitant of the town running from one end of Kirkwall to the other with the uppies (the people from one end of the town) competing against the downies (the people from the other end).

The book also includes many obscure customs – the pint ceremony from Lanark, for example, hunting the wren from Ireland and the Isle of Man (featured recently in *The Countryman*), New Year's Eve Fireballs from Stonehaven, near Aberdeen, and the summer birch from Glamorgan. My only quibble is that the book is hardly a good read – more a dictionary for those who'd like to go and see those customs that continue to be held.

Far more ancient are the farming customs discussed in Francis Pryor's meticulously researched **Farmers in Prehistoric Britain** (£14.99 from Tempus, The Mill, Brimscombe Port, Stroud, Glos tel 01453 883300, £14.99). Readers of *The Countryman* will know Dr Pryor from his regular column in the magazine and although this book is aimed at the expert there is much of interest for the enthusiastic amateur. Unlike most professional archeologists Dr Pryor is a farmer and this gives him a practical edge when it comes to archaeology. He tries to answer such fascinating questions as: ' What is it like to fetch primitive sheep with a dog?' 'How easy is it to split timber using wedges?' and 'Was it easier to build turf-roofed or thatched roundhouses?'.

Building styles and our attitude to them is the subject of Timothy Mow's fascinating **Stylistic Cold Wars** (John Murray, £14.99) which charts the long-running dispute between architectural historian Nikolaus Pevsner (1903-1983) and poet laureate John Betjeman (1906-1984). Pevsner, as readers will know, produced his monumental *The Buildings of England*, but was an unashamed apologist for the modernist movement in architecture. Betjeman, on the other hand, loathed the kind of steel and glass boxes that did more damage to (for example) historic London than all the bombs dropped during the Blitz. My sympathies are entirely with Betjeman on this one and I've always felt that Pevsner made himself ridiculous by listing brutal tower blocks by architects like Richard Seifert alongside masterpieces by Wren and Hawksmoor.

Betjeman's campaign against the wholesale redevelopment of the centres of our old towns and cities, his romantic view that old buildings, whatever their architectural merit, have a value simply because they are old has only recently come to be generally accepted. For years he was up against modernists who argued (and still do) that to wish to preserve old buildings is to indulge in foolish sentimentality. While the modernists held sway in the 1960s beautiful ancient buildings were swept away with impunity; thanks to John Betjeman and others like him we now realise that ancient villages and towns are best left as they are.

The history of buildings forms part of Alan Palmer's fascinating new book **The East End** (John Murray, £10.99). Many readers will say 'Why are you reviewing a book about London in *The Countryman*?' My answer is that the book takes us back to the time when the East End was made up of tiny villages – the original Tower Hamlets – and farms. Mr Palmer's book is a very good, well researched read. In it we discover how the docks that turned Britain into the world's richest

Swans over marsh marigolds: this splendid photograph is just one of more than 100 superb wildlife shots from all over the world from Heather Angels' new book Natural Visions (Collins and Brown £17.99). The book includes lots of practical tips about how the different photographs were taken.

The Rill, Shute House, Wiltshire from Jane Brown's The English Garden Through the 20th Century. See Val Bourne's review on page 109.

trading nation were built; how the East End was once famous for its cream and cherries (according to Samuel Pepys) and how the spirit of the East End – so heavily bombed during the war – came to symbolise the indomitable spirit of the British in general at times of national emergency.

By way of complete contrast, Kathryn Bradley-Hole's **Garden Lover's Guide to Britain** (BBC Worldwide, £12.99) has just reached a second edition. First published in 1998 the book covers gardens big and small pretty much from Land's End to John O'Groats with details of opening times, entrance fees and clear how-to-get-there details.

Anyone who doubts the importance of footpaths through the countryside should study Kim Taplin's book, **The English Path** (Perry Green Press – tel 01787 313853), now in its second edition. Mr Taplin looks at how the path was seen by writers and artists including Hardy and Jane Austen and how it

cemented together the lives of villagers in the days before the coming of the motor car.

Neil Grant's **Scottish Clans and Tartans** (Hamlyn, £12.99) is a no-nonsense guide to who wears what from Abercromby to Wemyss. Each section includes an excellent colour photograph of the tartan in question and a history of the family and its name.

•••••••••••••••••••••••••••••••

Stranger in our midst
Humphrey Phelps on a new biography of Laurie Lee

Laurie Lee: the Well-loved **Stranger** by Valerie Grove (Viking, £20) is the authorised biography of the author of *Cider With Rosie*. Mrs Grove had access to all Lee's diaries and correspondence, and quotes from them extensively. Her title is well chosen. Laurie Lee was well-loved by everyone – well, almost everyone. Some of the praise by his friends is fulsome, but he was also secretive, even to the point of deceit, weaving and living in a fantasy world. His autobiographic books owe as much to fantasy as to fact.

Valerie Grove, with great skill has unravelled much of the tangle and produced an absorbing book on this author, poet, broadcaster and play-wright – a man more at home in the Chelsea Arts Club than the

Cotswolds. Incidentally, where did she hear that Painswick, next to Slad, was devastated by bombs during the war?

This is a sympathetic biography. She gives credit to his work and makes valiant arguments in his defence. But she does not overlook his blemishes, which were many. He emerges as a poseur and a show-off and like Carroll and Kilvert, he was fascinated by young girls. He had a long affair with a married woman by whom he had a daughter who was brought up by the woman's husband. Eventually he married another mistress's teenage daughter, and when she had a daughter he wrote a book about her called *The Firstborn*.

'Charm', Lee wrote in 1978, 'is the ultimate weapon, the supreme, against which there are few defences. If you've got it, you need almost nothing else, neither money, looks, nor pedigree'. As Mrs Grove remarks, he was 'a supreme practitioner of the art of effortless attraction; men, women and children fell under his spell and part of his appeal was his boyishness'. Until he hit the jackpot with *Cider With Rosie*, the bubble that never burst, he had very little money and to some extent relied on the generosity of his friends. He was less than generous to Wilma Gregory, his benefactress, and omitted any reference to her in his autobiography.

The account of his experience in the Spanish Civil War has been questioned. Mrs Grove says if it is untrue why did he invent it. The story was good enough without invention. I think the answer is that he could no longer tell fantasy from fact and if he lied it was because it was his nature to lie.

I finished the biography by feeling pity for Laurie Lee. All his life he suffered from epileptic fits, from fevers and late in life a non-malignant growth which made it difficult for him to eat or taste anything. A life of heavy drinking took its toll, he became deaf and his eyesight failed. Then he had cancer of the bowel which eventually killed him.

Valerie Grove has gathered a vast amount of facts about this charming but tormented man. And having gathered them, felt constrained to use them, relevant or not. Consequently the book is too long (over 500 pages) and there were occasions when I skipped a few paragraphs. However, she has written a splendid biography. Whether it will please all Laurie Lee's many fans I cannot say, but it did make me start to re-read *Cider With Rosie* and re-visit the Slad Valley.

....

Walk this way
Elizabeth Steward discovers some themed trails

Does anyone ever actually use large format general walking books – they're too big even to keep in the car – or are they always consigned to the bookshelf for reference? The AA have sorted out this problem in a neat way with their new **Book of Britain's Walks** (AA Publishing, £30) which comes complete with a pocket book of

An engraving of George Bennet from Tom Hiney's new book On the Missionary Trail (Chatto £17.99). Bennet and his colleague Daniel Tyerman were sent in 1821 to visit Christian missionary stations in the most remote parts of the world. Over the next eight years they travelled 80,000 miles often in the most harrowing conditions. What is most interesting about this new book is its revelation that, contrary to modern thinking, many 19th century missionaries were not ranting religious zealots; many did a great deal of practical good among very poor people.

directions and maps for 120 easy circular walks all over Britain.

The beautiful photographs really show the diversity of our landscapes, and each walk takes a particular theme – literary, geological, historic, and so on – for added interest. A small location map for each one would have been useful, but apart from that it's a lovely book for dipping into and planning family outings.

....

Gripping yarns
Michelle Corps on a new book by birdwatcher Bill Oddie

Gripping Yarns, Tales of Birds & Birding (Christopher Helm, £7.99) is a brilliant collection of more than 60 magazine pieces by Bill Oddie.

Compiled from over five years work, the articles used are the pre-published originals, and therefore the book includes much previously unseen material. Oddie captures the reader's interest by explaining how his fascination with birds started, and secures it with madcap tips on how to avoid other birders, and stump over-talkative cab drivers.

Gripping Yarns is as much an entertaining autobiography as an excellent insight into the highs and lows of birding – and it's packed full of anecdotes that had me cackling out loud and practising 'pishing'. To find out what that means you'll have to read the book! My only regret is that some of the terms are not explained for non-birders – but that is only the tiniest of complaints, as I'd recommend this book to enthusiasts and non enthusiasts alike.

A Stroll in the Country (£5.99 from Powdene Publicity Ltd, Unit 17, St Peter's Wharf, Newcastle upon Tyne, NE6 1TZ) by Henry Brewis is a collection of amusing stories about rural life, awkward animals and country characters. Good to dip in to, I liked it, although some might find it a bit risqué in places. Just re-released, **The Revised**

Pocket Dictionary of The Horse (£5.99 from Tabb House, 7 Church Street, Padstow, Cornwall, PL28 8BG) covers almost every horse and riding term, offers advice on careers with horses and now includes updated entries on veterinary matters.

....

Great gardens
Val Bourne takes a few short cuts

Christopher Lloyd owns one of the best gardens in England – Great Dixter in East Sussex. In spring wild orchids pepper the dry moat and sweeps of tulips and wallflowers mingle. But the real impact hits you from mid-summer onwards, when strong colours (lots of yellow and orange especially) and tall exuberant plants with stark shapes tower above you in the Long Border. **Lloyd's Garden Flowers** (Cassell, £30) dispenses a whole range of plant knowledge gathered from a lifetime's gardening experience. Set out in alphabetical order, it covers perennials, bulbs, grasses and ferns. This is a book to keep, and use again and again.

The refreshing honesty of Christopher Lloyd's writing – a man of strong opinions – describes each plant's good and bad points. This is going to be a gardening classic for all gardeners, be they experienced or novice.

Short Cuts to Beautiful Gardens by David Squire (Ward Lock, £16.99) is a practical book that deals with improving your garden by building pergolas, arches, paths, border edgings, herb gardens etc, without spending a fortune. Although there are lots of labour saving and money saving tips and plant lists, the plant information is rather sketchy. Blue flowers are listed, but without a clear indication of which need sun or shade, or when they flower. This is a book for do-it-yourself gardeners with a small garden, rather than the serious plant lover.

I'm delighted to say that there seems to be a move away from the coffee table garden book written round sets of photographs, to well researched text. **The English Garden Through the 20th Century** (Garden Art Press, £25) is a revised second edition. It begins with Gertrude Jekyll's Munstead Wood garden and goes through the Arts and Craft Movement, Italianate gardens, the Modern and Post-Modern Movement and Geoffrey Jellicoe's design philosophy. It also covers Hidcote, Sissinghurst and Rodmarton Manor (a Gloucestershire Arts and Craft garden).

Each of the ten chapters is packed with information, illustrated by old photographs and plans and gives us fascinating insights into each garden or garden style. Although many of the gardens featured are very well known they are dealt with in great depth, throwing up lots of new information. An academic book for the dedicated garden visitor and the student of garden history.

Looking at nature

Peter Marren on what makes good conservation

Greg Dyke, the incoming head of the BBC, says he wants to take resources away from 'management' and devote them to making better television programmes. I wonder whether our official nature conservation bodies will take notice and follow suit. For what seems a long time now, English Nature and its sister bodies in Scotland and Wales, have seemed more interested in management than in wildlife. The most visible sign of this has been streams of strategies, guidelines and business plans in which commonplace observations alternate with the most impenetrable gobbledegook. I doubt whether our experienced and country-wise wildlife charities and pressure groups are much in need of all this boring advice.

In a saner world, English Nature would instead channel most of its annual budget of £40 million into the private sector without delay, keeping only enough reserves in hand to reward deserving farmers and smallholders. Its main task would be to ensure the money went where it was most needed, and to that end it would have good people out in the country who know their patch inside out, and are not moved around every couple of years as a 'career move'.

As it happens, English Nature is now under new management, under Barbara Young, who used to head the RSPB, and David Arnold-Forster, formerly in charge of the North Yorks Moors National Parks Authority. I know nothing about Arnold-Forster, but Barbara is really rather interesting, with a pretty wit, outspoken where she needs to be and a good political head on her shoulders. She also happens to be a governor of the BBC. We must wait with interest to see whether the new brooms decide to take a leaf out of the BBC's book and remove resources from 'management' in order to devote them to conserving wildlife.

One of the main problems for nature conservation today is that so few people seem to have much idea about what needs doing. My newspaper recently asked some intelligent children what their main concerns were. The answers were GM food, cruelty to animals, fox-hunting and the right to roam (they were respectively against, against, against and for). But although these are the issues that make the headlines, they have very little to do with insuring the way of life of, say, a butterfly or a newt. They are not really conservation issues.

By the same token, many of these same children equated nature conservation with protecting or planting trees. In my experience no single fact is harder to get over than

David Kjaer

most of our remaining natural woodlands need is more felling, not less (and then left to regenerate naturally). Still, what do you expect from an authority whose woodland is the responsibility of a Heritage and Urban Design department. To planners, a tree isn't a living plant, rather a kind of leafy decoration.

The first spring flowers are appearing here, on the sheltered, sunny banks of Ramsbury, with the celandines, or 'swallow herbs', heralding the season of growth and renewal.

that trees in the wrong place are bad for wildlife. Take two recent cases. Alan Titchmarsh, the popular TV gardener, has a big sycamore in his garden that he wants to chop down and the local council won't let him. And in the London Borough of Bromley, they are similarly blocking the felling of some oak trees for an archaeological project. The facts – that sycamore is an absolute menace in our native woods and that nature benefits from sound woodland practice, including the thinning and felling of oaks – are less persuasive than the myth that nature conservation means Hands Off the Trees. What

I wonder whether the difficulty many people seem to have in naming our once familiar wild flowers stems from field guides – in which each plant is shown against a black background, plucked, as it were, from its natural place. How sweeter and truer to nature were the old Ladybird books, which showed mallows and pennywort sprouting through ruined stones, poppies and campions edging the fields where stooks of corn dry in the sun, and harebells and heaths in the lea of an upland tarn. What flowers look like is only half their charm. Where they grow is just as important – and beguiling. ■

Plaid, truis and tartans

Ivor Smullen with a brief history of Scotland's national dress

Not long ago a woollen factory on Tayside was working flat out to produce an order for 2,500 tartan kilts and mini-kilts for women in Japan. The firm described the tartan business as 'quite amazing'. They also handled orders from the United States and Canada, where there are an estimated 30 million people of Scottish descent, keen to wear their clan tartans at every opportunity.

The word 'tartan' was in use at least as early as the 16th century, although the kilt as we know it now is largely a 19th century invention. The original Highland tartan was the plaid, a long piece of cloth woven from the wool of native sheep and dyed with leaves, berries, bark and lichens.

The word 'plaid' has no certain origin, but it is probably connected with the Irish word *ploid* for blanket. Donning the plaids, as it was called, was no mean feat. First a fellow laid the plaid – all six yards of it – on the ground with a belt beneath. He would then pleat it halfway across its width. Next he would wrap the material round his waist like a skirt, and then throw the remainder, as it were, over his shoulder. This precarious sounding garment was held in place by a belt.

The plaid was eventually adapted to assume roughly the form of the modern kilt. One story has it that an English furnace-master in Scotland felt that the original long plaid was an industrial hazard, deserving to be cut down on those grounds alone.

Highlanders also wore trews (originally *truis*), a form of tartan trousers rather like leggings, together with a belted plaid. Soldiers of some Scots regiments still wear tartan trousers.

Tartan's dark days came during the 18th-century Jacobite risings. The Highland clansmen so frightened the government in England that, when they were finally defeated at the bloody battle of Culloden (1746), fierce reprisals were carried out. One was a ban on tartan dress, imposed on all except those in the army who had remained loyal to the English cause.

Suspected Jacobites were asked to take an oath never to 'use any tartan, plaid or any part of the Highland garb' on pain of being cursed. The ban lasted for 35 years, not being lifted until it became clear that the Jacobite claims to the British throne were no longer a significant threat. The only dissenting voice was that of one Sir Philip Jennings Clarke, who wanted

Highland dress to be confined to Scotland because of the experience of an English innkeeper, whose wife and daughters were allegedly attracted to the tartans of four Highland officers billeted on them.

The end of the tartan ban led to wide rejoicing. A Highland proclamation announced: 'Listen, men! This is bringing before all the Sons of Gael that the King and Parliament of Britain have for ever abolished the Act against Highland Dress; which came down to the clans from the beginning of the world to the year 1746. You are no longer bound to the unmanly dress of the Lowlander. This is declaring to every man, young and old, single and gentle, that they may after this put on and wear the truis, the little kilt, the coat and the striped hose, as also the belted plaid without fear of the law of the realm or the spite of enemies'.

Two-and-a-half centuries later, the sideways-kicking step of Highland dancers is said to symbolise the kicking off of trousers in favour of the kilt.

By Victorian times, tartan had become so popular that it was worn at high society balls, both in Britain and abroad. Meanwhile military tailoring had a smartening-up effect on Highland dress, the coloured stripes falling exactly on the fold of the pleat.

An Aberdeen law student, James Logan, carried out a study of tartans that produced a level of standardisation. Trudging the length and breadth of Scotland, he collected tartan specimens, eventually publishing a book about them. The origins he gave for some tartans were condemned as inspired guesswork, but there was no doubt about the cloth's overall popularity.

Tartan was used not only for

Four Highlanders: the two outer figures are dressed in the shoulder plaid, the second from the left in trews, the other in the belted-plaid.

plaid, but for shawls, blankets and tablecloths. Even boxes, tins and dishes with tartan designs were produced and despatched to eager customers overseas. According to one account, slaves in the West Indies were forced to wear brightly-coloured tartan shawls so that they could be easily spotted if they ran away.

The pattern was made even more desirable by the romantic writings of Sir Walter Scott, who masterminded George IV's visit to Edinburgh in 1822: an occasion for great celebration. Heads of families swathed themselves in tartan, much of dubious authenticity. The portly Lord Mayor of London, who took part in the proceedings, was so carried away by the festive atmosphere, that he stripped off his tartan costume to dance naked down Princes Street.

Despite this ill-considered behaviour, the event placed tartan firmly in the mainstream of Scottish culture, leading to the evolution of the kilt as the national costume.

Greenhouse

Proffered as a gift for my fortieth birthday,
at first I resisted, considered alternatives:
the 'good coat' I'd never had, a decent typewriter –
resented the implication of devils and idle hands,
of being 'done good to' – the only daughter who still
couldn't drive, whose 'artistic promise' had faltered.

Three days he struggled to put it up:
cementing paving slabs into a solid base,
connecting the frame, clipping shivery glass –
the last in teeming rain, a cut thumb
wrapped in his handkerchief.

Which left nothing to do but start...
press compost and sharp sand into seed-trays,
plant, prick out, lift into pots, grobags,
fasten with string and canes the way he taught me,
prune, feed, spray, rub out sideshoots,
thumbs pungent with Alicante, Aisla Craig;
the air rich with coriander, marigolds.

Patricia Pogson

Whatever happened to Poppyland?

Bel Bailey on the fate of a Norfolk legend

Can there still be a bottle of 'Poppyland Bouquet' perfume hidden away in some Norfolk attic? Made by Daniel Davison of Cromer, it was sold all over the world from 1890 until 1930. Poppyland china was also the name given to a range of Staffordshire china. Nowadays nobody seems able even to describe this intriguing product. Surely it was not *all* smashed over the years?

In the 19th century, Poppyland was one of Britain's most popular destinations. But today few could even tell you where it was...

Its strange story began with Clement Scott, a *Daily Telegraph* journalist who arrived at Cromer on August 1, 1883. He thought the town very pretty, but disliked the crowds and strolled off in search of solitude along the cliff top.

The scarlet poppies at Sidestrand attracted him, especially those growing near a neglected old graveyard on the cliffs with a picturesque crumbling church tower brooding over it.

This set the writer's imagination to work at once and inspired a whole series of articles. These Scott called Poppyland – by a holiday-maker, written at a farmhouse by the sea.

His dramatic style of writing was immensely popular with those late Victorian readers who clamoured for more and a volume entitled *Poppyland Papers* appeared in 1886. His poem *The Garden of Sleep* had a kind of melancholy yearning, typical of that age. It was set to music and became one of the hit songs of the time. One verse ran:

In my garden of sleep, where red
 poppies are spread,
I wait for the living, alone with the
 dead!
For a flower in ruins stands guard
 o'er the deep,
At whose feet are green graves of
 dear women asleep!
Did they love, as I love when they
 lived by the sea?
Did they wait, as I wait, for the days
 that may be?
Was it in hope or fulfilling, that
 entered each breast,
Ere death gave release, and the
 poppies gave rest?...
Sleep, my Poppyland, sleep!'

To modern tastes this is rather morbid stuff but Scott's readers lapped it up avidly. Floods of letters

The fame of Poppyland had a commercial value too: with wealthy and talented Londoners buying up property, Cromer and the surrounding areas became increasingly prosperous.

wanted to know what had inspired the lyrics. Then he explained the fascination the old churchyard held for him and that the poppies symbolised death. Strangely his readers wanted to see the spot for themselves, and the whole area became popular with visitors less morbid than Scott and determined to enjoy themselves.

So, Poppyland was originally Sidestrand and nearby Overstrand, but, coupled with the opening of the railway to North Norfolk, Scott's articles made the whole area round Cromer synonymous with the name Poppyland. A local railway company even opened a 'Poppy-line' from Cromer to Mundesley, and a hotel boom followed in the 1890s to accommodate the many visitors. Railway advertisements also boosted the poppyland theme so the area became famous.

In his writings Scott referred to 'the farmhouse by the sea'– in reality Mill House was at Overstrand, where he stayed with the miller and his daughter Louie Jermy – whose blackberry puddings and jams became famous after Scott's friends praised them so warmly. Louie was the 'Maid of the Mill' to whom the book *Poppyland* was dedicated. Probably the 42-year-old Scott (at the time of their first meeting) was more than a little in love with the much younger Louie, an attractive brunette. Louie revelled in the influx of the famous to Poppyland as she especially enjoyed the company of poets, actors and authors.

Some of these wealthy and talented Londoners had houses built in Poppyland which led to increasing prosperity for the villagers. In fact Overstrand a century ago, became known as 'The Village of Millionaires' as Lord and Lady Battersea bought a house there, followed by Sir Edgar Speyer, Sir George Lewis and Sir John Hare who all built new houses, or bought existing large ones.

At this period, around the turn of the century, Overstrand's population increased to over 400 (from 253). Cromer's population more than doubled to 3,781 by

Clement Scott – the writer and poet who immortalised Poppyland.

1901, and even Sheringham benefited from the new railway link, and its population increased by more than 300 in those early Poppyland years.

Famous visitors to Miller Jermy's home included the poet Swinburne, his great friend Watts-Dunton, George Sims (famous for his ballad *Christmas Day in the Workhouse*) also the great actor Henry Irving. While at Poppyland, Swinburne wrote *A Midsummer Holiday*, Sims often praised it in his columns in *The Referee* and Watts-Dunton wrote *Aylwin*, all while staying at the Mill House, so there was clearly some magic at

The Garden of Sleep

Central to the image of Poppyland were the drowsy fields of flowers and the tower overlooking the sea.

work in Poppyland. The next to 'discover' the area was the artist W.W. Russell sent hot foot in 1893 to Overstrand by the *Lady's Pictorial*. This resulted in the book *Vera in Poppyland*!

'Scottomania' was established so well by now that souvenirs and postcards of the area were much sought after. These would form a very interesting collection but one rarely comes across them today.

Even as late as 1923, when Clement Scott had already been dead for 19 years, the *Westminster Gazette!* stated that 'Cromer stands as the metropolis of Poppyland', but

soon the guide books left out the captivating word as the vivid image faded.

Clement Scott died in 1904, his beloved old tower at Sidestrand toppled over the cliffs in 1916 and poor Louie was evicted from her beloved home in 1919 – though she lived in a Tower Lane cottage until her death in 1934 – the last of the legends of Poppyland.

Still left, however, is the Clement Scott memorial standing at the entrance to Poppyland on the road between Cromer and Overstrand. As you visit it remember that near here a famous dream was born... ∎

The Countryman

Hotels and Guest Houses

COTSWOLDS

BEAUTIFULLY APPOINTED ground-floor B&B accommodation in quiet village house near Bampton. En-suite, superb breakfast, parking. ETB 4 diamonds From £18pppn. Brochure tel/fax 01993 841368.

CUMBRIA & THE LAKES

Clare House
Park Road, Grange-over-Sands
Cumbria LA11 7HQ
Telephone: (015395) 33026

Wake to feel the warmth of the morning sun in your room as it rises above the hills beyond, admire the view across the bay . . . relax a while with your paper or take a stroll along the promenade before enjoying your breakfast, cooked as you would like it, with fresh-baked croissants, home-made marmalade and have a leisurely day in the Lakes, returning to a delightful dinner. Tempted?
We will be pleased to see you.
Re-opening April 1st with early season terms until May 27th eg any 4 days £174.00 DB&B
Proprietors: D. S. & J. Read.
ETB 🌟🌟🌟 *Highly Commended.* AA ★ 76% 🏆

DEVON

Toad Hall Cottages
150 outstanding waterside and rural properties in truly beautiful locations in Devon and Dorset.
For our Brochure Call
01548 853777
(24 Hours)

EAST DEVON (COLYTON). Excellent walking in lovely secluded valleys, 4 miles sea (Beer). B&B £14 a day, Winter £84 weekly, Summer £91 weekly, H. tea extra. Tel:01404 871251

SOUTHERNMOST DEVON

Small Country Hotel magnificently situated in six acres of mature gardens overlooking the panorama of Slapton Ley Nature Reserve and Start bay. Coastal and rural walks of outstanding natural beauty. All rooms overlook the sea. AA & RAC* Also four self-contained bungalows. Greyhomes Hotel, Torcross, Near Kingsbridge, South Devon. Tel: Kingsbridge 01548 580 220

DERBYSHIRE

DERBYSHIRE Quiet accommodation offered at this part Elizabethan Manor Farmhouse, which is situated in an unspoilt hamlet near Matlock. En-suite rooms, all centrally heated. Cosy sitting room, and separate dining room . Three Les Routiers awards. Tel 01629 534246

DORSET

LYME REGIS 3 miles. NON SMOKING two star hotel offering superb home cooking & accom. (incl ground floor). Ideal walking (nr coast path), touring, NT, gardens & fossil hunting. (01297 442972)

HEREFORDSHIRE

PEACEFUL 17THC RESTORED barn near Hay on Wye, superb views, B&B £18.00. Details Tel 01497 831690

SHROPSHIRE

SHROPSHIRE B&B. Stay in historic hall in heart of Welsh Marches near Ludlow (no pets). Mrs Watkins, Broadward Hall, CLUNGUNFORD, CRAVEN ARMS, SY7 0QA. Tel: 01547 530 357.

SOMERSET

SOMERSET Easy access Exmoor coast twinbed room BB EM opt: Non smoking: Peaceful location 01984 623591

SUFFOLK

WOODBRIDGE. B&B. Town centre, secluded excellent accommodation, en suite, with all facilities. Own parking. Non-smoking. From £20 pp. 01394 383416

YORKSHIRE

HELMSLEY, NORTH YORKSHIRE En suite farmhouse accommodation with beautiful views, delicious food. Highly Commended. 2 nights db & b £79.00. Tel:01439 798221

SLEIGHTS NEAR WHITBY. Peaceful surroundings and wonderful views. Home cooking, H&C. B&B, optional E.M. Mrs Nettleton, Wick Cottage, Carr Hill Lane, Sleights. Tel:01947 810664

WENSLEYDALE Take a break in this wonderful hidden village of Thoralby. B & B and dinner optional ETB 3 diamonds, farmhouse. Panoramic views, all rooms En-suite, children & pets welcome tel/fax 01969 663319

WALES

DEVILS BRIDGE Licensed Guest House. Superb cuisine, en suite, wonderful walks. Spectacular Birdlife. Log fires. Open all year. Informative Brochure tel: 01974 282289.

EXCELLENT 17THC Guest house plus self-catering cottage. 5 miles from beautiful Cardigan bay. Enquiries: Judith Russil, Rhydlewis House, Rhydlewis, near Llandysul Ceredigion SA44 5PE tel: 01239 851748

SEE UNDER GUESTHOUSES For 17thC self-catering cottage.

SNOWDONIA Country House B&B. Beautiful setting overlooking Betws-y-Coed and mountains. Quiet and comfortable. Non Smoking. Telephone for details 01690 710 440

SCOTLAND

Situated in "The Wild Garden of Skye" a short distance from the Ferry bringing you "Over the sea to Skye" and overlooking the Sound of Sleat with the Knoydart Mountains beyond...A superb Hotel offering Luxury En-suite facilities. Ideal for Walking, Fishing, Sailing etc.

3 ½ COMMENDED AA 1 ½TASTE OF SCOTLAND

Spring Breaks Available

For Brochure tel: 01471 844223 Fax: 01471 844495

GALLOWAY/SOUTH WEST COAST Luxurious Victorian country house, beautiful gardens, fine food. "Gulf-Stream" climate, spectacular scenery, rich heritage, quiet roads. Rowallan House STB 4-star B&B Tel: 01671 402520

SCOTTISH HIGHLANDS Inverewe Garden 6 miles. Small guesthouse near sea/mountains. Non-smoking. Home cooking. STB 3 Stars. En-suite rooms. Brochure. Aultbea 01445 731375.

STRATHPEFFER LUXURY B&B In Victorian Spa village ideally situated for touring Scottish Highlands. En-suite, parking, non-smoking. Please phone 01997 420118

HOTELS AND GUEST HOUSES

EAST DEVON HAMLET Weston, peaceful thatched cottage for B&B. Woodland and cliff top walks with abundant wildlife. Brochure 01395 512238

HOLIDAYS FURTHER AFIELD

ALPUJARRA SOUTHERN SPAIN Holiday cottage sleeps 4 10km from coast peaceful village birdwatching, walking, scenic 01756 790797 or 0403 474 881

CENTRAL FRANCE Argueton-sur-Creuse. B&B in comfortable, modernised farmhouse. English proprietors. Excellent stopover/centre in beautiful country rich in birdlife or try something different with a Falconry course. Tel: 0033 25424 0776

CENTRAL BRITTANY Comfortable well equipped Breton cottage. Sleeps 4/5. Some dates except July/August. Details Tel: 0033 296 457334 Fax: 0033 296 457707.

PROVENCE, CAMARGUE Farm Cottage, Also B&B. Rogers, Mas d'Auphan, Le Sambuc, 13200 Arles, France. Tel: 0033 490972041 Fax: 490972087

HOLIDAYS

CRUISE THROUGH THE COUNTRYSIDE aboard our owner hosted Hotel Narrow Boats on the canals and rivers of England and Wales. Enjoy peaceful countryside, walking and fine home cooking. Single/ Twin and Double en-suite cabins available for 7 night cruises. Inland Waterway Holiday Cruises, Greenham Lock Cottage, London Road, Newbury, Berkshire RG14 5SN Tel 07831 110811 Fax 07767 669045 (mob).Internet:http:// www.bargeholidayuk.com

OXFORDSHIRE NARROW-BOATS. For a friendly, peaceful holiday, cruise the beautiful rural Oxford Canal/Upper Thames. Top quality, centrally heated, 2-12 berth narrowboats. Also day boats. For a free brochure phone 01869 340348. Canal Wharf, Lower Heyford, Oxfordshire OX6 3PD

SELF CATERING HOLIDAYS

CORNWALL

HELFORD RIVER COTTAGE Durgan sleeps 5/8, tv, ch. Close to beach and coastal walks, boats and sailboards nearby. All Year. Falmouth 01326 250119

NORTH CORNWALL cosy cottage for 2 on peaceful small farm close to Boscastle & coastal paths. Two other cottages for 4 Telephone St Gennys (01840) 230470 for brochure.

WATERSIDE COTTAGE or part of manor house. Central location. CH, open fire, 4-poster bed. Substantial gardens. Unspoilt views. Boat available. Tel: 01208 872444

COTSWOLDS

'COTTAGE IN THE COUNTRY'. Delightful holiday homes - Heart of England, Cotswolds,Shropshire, Windsor etc. Comfort, quality & value, Broch: 01993 831495. cottage@cotswold0.demon.co.uk

DELIGHTFUL GROUND FLOOR Flat in rural location near Bampton. Linen, C.H., parking, non-smoking. Weekly from £150. Details tel/fax 01993 841368.

MORETON-IN-MARSH Cottage sleeps 3 CH col TV no pets Tel: 01608 650666

NR CHIPPING NORTON S/C Flat in converted watermill. Beautiful isolated setting. Fully equipped. Sleeps 2. Brochure Tel: 01608 686537

CUMBRIA & THE LAKES

AMBLESIDE. Traditional stone house, sleeps 6, pets welcome, peaceful with lovely views, terraced garden. Tel: 0208 392 1285

TWO'S COMPANY Renovated rural cottage for two in South Lakeland. Ideal base for walking, touring or sailing; 3-acre Yellow Book garden Regret no pets. From £130/week. Tel: (Windermere) 015394 46238

DERBYSHIRE

TIDESWELL COSY COTTAGE Sleeps 5 from £150 central heating & electricity included telephone 01433 639719

DEVON

CREDITON SPACIOUS WING Lovely historic farmhouse. Beautiful grounds, woods, river. Children warmly welcomed. Excellent touring centre. Mrs Mills. Tel: 01363 83268

SECLUDED Waterside cottage, idyllic setting near Salcombe. Also attractive rural retreats, swimming pool, tennis courts etc. Discount sometimes available for OAPs. Full colour brochure Tel: Toad Hall Cottages 01548 853089

WATERSIDE COTTAGES In Looe/Fowey/Polruan. Superb views. Dinghies available. Pets welcome. Area of outstanding natural beauty. Open all year. (01579) 344667

DORSET

17TH-CENTURY THATCHED COTTAGE. Village near Bridport. Sleeps 2. Log fire, linen, no pets/ smokers. Tel 01308 897716.

LINCOLNSHIRE

EDGE OF WOLDS Secluded cottage in peaceful garden sleeps 2-3 01790 752477

EXMOOR

EXMOOR The Pack Horse Holiday Flats in N.T. village of Allerford are ideally suited for 2/3 persons seeking peace in countryside untouched by time.
Open all year. C/Heated ETC ꙮ commended. Safe parking. Family cottage available. B&B. Short breaks.
Brochure by return Tel/Fax 01643 862475

HAMPSHIRE

NEAR NEW FOREST Charming thatched cottage fully equipped sleeps 4, spacious garden, parking, conservation village 01788 543932

NORFOLK

CHARMING SMALL COTTAGE Near Sandringham and coast open fire from £160 per week Tel 01159 258235

MID-NORFOLK LUXURY Rural bungalow, sleeps 6/cots, 4-poster, en-suite, whirlpool bath, bodyjet shower, CH, children/pets welcome, non-smokers, private garden/parking. Tel: 01953 851042

SHROPSHIRE

SHROPSHIRE, BISHOP'S CASTLE Stately home: spacious flat, splendid surroundings. Ideal children. 41 Cheval place, London, SW7 1EW. Tel: 0171 581 2782

WENLOCK EDGE. PEACEFUL Comfortable single storey cottage for 2 C/H, TV. ꙮ commended. Tel: 01694 771286

SOMERSET

LUXURY COTTAGES
Quantock hills conservation village centre. Sleeps 2/3. Fully equipped, walled garden. tel 01278 732 392

SUFFOLK

LAVENHAM. Delightful Victorian cottage, edge medieval village, sleeps three. Exceptionally well-equipped. CH/linen. Secluded garden. Picturesque countryside. Over 60s reductions. No smokers/pets. Tel: 01284 828428.

SOUTHWOLD Suffolk House, S/c flats, immaculate, full linen, colour TV, etc. Sea views. Sleeps 2-4. Also pretty cottage and bungalow in charming village. All personally supervised. Available all year. Tel: Southwold 01502 723742

SUSSEX

EAST SUSSEX-SEDLESCOMBE- Delightful converted stableblock. Rural location. Excellent base for towns, castles, gardens in "1066" country. Short breaks. Sleeps 2. Tel: 01424870362

WILTSHIRE

COUNTRY HOUSE ANNEXE Lovely surroundings, garden, pets, N/s. Sleeps 2/4. Tel 01380 813304

YORKSHIRE

NORTH YORK MOORS and coast award winning stone cottages from £180/week. Quiet wooded setting. Open all year. Short breaks and riding available. Brochure 01723 859019

WHITBY QUALITY FLATS From £100 pw sleep 2-5 5mins sea, harbour, shops, restaurants. Brochure Tel/Fax 01947 604213

WALES

BREATHTAKING VIEWS Over Morpha Harlech. Very comfortable 3-bedroomed detached house in own grounds Harlech 1 1/12 miles, Porth Madoc 10, Barmouth 12 miles phone for brochure 01352 756076

NORTH PEMBROKESHIRE FARM Two miles coast, comfortable, peaceful, centrally heated accommodation. Pets welcome, available all year. Joyce Lorenz tel 01239 881688.

IDYLLIC SECLUDED cottage (sleeps 2-4) near Devil's Bridge. Stunning scenery, walking, birdwatching. C/h. Dogs welcome. Tel: 01981 250849/01974 282631

MID-WALES Elan Valley. Converted granary(4), cottage(7) on remote smallholding bordering moorland and RSPB reserve. Peaceful. Unspoilt. 01597 810120

NORTH WALES Near Abersoch attractive quiet seaside cottage, meadow. Sleeps six open-fire pets welcome 01507 604408

ROCH, PEMBROKESHIRE. Five double bedroom cottage. Spacious, comfortable, large garden, close beach, secluded. Tel: 01635 201218.

WELSH BORDER Unspoilt countryside surrounds our luxury, secluded farm cottage. Accommodating 2-7 +. Pets Welcome 01544 260237

SCOTLAND

LITHMORE ARGYLL Ideal for a quiet relaxing holiday on this lovely island. Fully equipped cottage Brochure 01631 760247

SCOTTISH BORDERS Morebattle near Kelso carefully restored cottage for two in centre of lovely village Tel: 01835 862310 for brochure

ISLE OF WIGHT

BRIGHTSTONE Luxury country cottage, idyllic situation, sea, downs. Sleeps 5. Tel 01983 740021.

ALMOST ANY BOOK Found. Free search, no obligation. Pickwick Books, Lavender Cottage, Shutlanger, Northamptonshire NN12 7RR

FREE BOOKSEARCH Most titles found. Details to: Mrs M.B. Skellern, 1 Dobbin Close, Cropwell Bishop, Notts NG12 3GR Tel: 0115 9892068

FREE LIST OF Second-hand/Out of Print Crime Fiction Books available from R. Andrews, 'The Barn', Brockhampton, Near Cheltenham, Glos.

H.P. BOOKFINDERS. Established professional service, no obligation, no SAE required. 22 Fords Close, Bledlow Ridge, Bucks HP14 4AP. Tel/Fax: 01494 481 118.

UNABLE TO OBTAIN a book you want? Free booksearch. No obligation. Sae for details. Find That book (Dept CM), 74 Oxford Avenue, Guiseley, LS20 9BX. 01943 872699 evenings

BUSINESS OPPORTUNITIES

EXTRA INCOME? Beehive makers seek local distributors throughout Britain. No cold selling involved, beekeeping experience not required. Please call 01661 886219 (day or evening) or send S.A.E. to Stamfordham Ltd FREEPOST NEA 1272 Newcastle-Upon-Tyne NE18 0BR for full details,

CHINA MATCHING

DENBY/LANGLEY. Discontinued Tableware bought and sold. Many designs in stock from, 1950/98 period. Tel: 01384 277849 email: denby.langley@ cableinet.co.uk

PERSONAL

FOR FREE REPORT On men's health write to Mr Barrett, 19 wheatfield Way, Brighton, BN2 4RQ

Lord of the Manor Titles
Heritage Brokers
FOR SALE BY PRIVATE TREATY
Inheritable, Valuable, Lordship of the Manor Titles.
Dating from 1066 a.d. or earlier.

Custom and Practice form of address: 'Lord & Lady' (spouse becomes 'Lady' on the acquisition of a Lordship of the Manor Title.)

Experience the difference a little can make.

Contact us in strictest confidence on:
Tel: 01628 850 562
Fax: 01628 527 623

PENFRIENDS MAKE NEW FRIENDS and good friends. Details SAE LINK LINE (CM) Box 7358 London N15QF

RICHARD JEFFRIES SOCIETY. Enquiries to Membership Secretary, 23 Hardwell Close, Grove, Wantage, Oxon OX120BN Tel. 012357 65360

CLOTHING AND FOOTWEAR

Lingerie
A wonderful collection
~ Ballet, Berlei, Barbara, Triumph, Sloggi etc. – in a wide range of sizes
Call for a FREE brochure
AMPLE♥BOSOM
01439 798388
www.bras-online.co.uk
email: amplebosom@ bras-online.co.uk

ALMOST UNWEAROUTABLE SOCKS and Shooting Socks, jerseys fairisle, etc, knitted to order. Write for details: Nicholl Knitwear, The Lodge, Highfield, Whittonstall, Consett, Co Durham DH8 9L2. Tel/Fax: 01207 508950

DR MARTEN SHOES Black, Oxblood, Waxy, Nu Buck, Brogues. Brochure: Bernard Timson, 111 Hinckley Road, Earl Shilton, Leicester.01455 842208

FEEL THE COLD? Try the soft cosy comfort of angora thermal clothing (warmer than wool). Extensive colourful range including underwear. FREE colour catalogue. Orkney Angora, FREEPOST SCO2687 (Dept CM), Sandy, Orkney, KW17 2BR. Tel/Fax 01857 600421 (24 hours)

COURSES

WEEKEND ART COURSES In glorious Scottish Borders. Unique team teaching. SAE: EH45 ART GROUP. c/o 21 Gallowhill PEEBLES EH45 9BG (01721 721160)

WOODCARVING COURSES IN Devon. Pleasant studio with comfortable accommodation nearby. Maximum five students. Beginners especially welcomed. Sae details: Zoe Gertner, Puddleduck Farm, South Wonford, Holsworthy, Devon. Tel: 01409 261648

GARDENING

DEACON'S MILLENIUM APPLE Tree at discounted price. Apples/ Pears/ Peaches/ Plums. Medana soft fruits. Plus wide selection of family trees. Nuts grapes & hops. FREE Specialist Fruit Tree Catalogue. Deacons Nursery (TC), Godshill, Isle of Wight, PO38 3HW. Tel: 01983 840750, 01983 522243, Fax: 01983 523575

Advertisers Index

Achievements 30
Alan Raddon..................................1
Christies....................................41
Coach House 30
Cudworths...................................115
Countryman John OBC/126
David Nieper.........................IBC/126
Darlington Borough Council 1
Eagle products 30
Foam for Comfort IFC/115
Genuine Guernsey Knitwear.............1
Guild of Aid for Gentlepeople 44
John Boddys Fine Wood 30
John Goodwin 47
Joseph Turner...............................1
Le Tricoteur.................................1
NPK Ltd.....................................47
Pedometers 40
Pentland Press 30
Rainbow Flowers 7
Rainmac.....................................47
Ribble Valley...............................1
Smith Ross Shane Insurance 66
Stamford Smokers 40
Swaledale 1
Taylor & Cross 40
The Countryman Binders................66
The Memoir Club 30
The Original No Elastic Socks.........40
The Publishing House 19
Windjammer Cruises 1

ORDER FORM for Pure Cotton Nightwear

Style No	Garment	Length	Price	S	M	L	XL	2XL	3XL
V 0082	Nightdress	48" long	£59						
		54" long	£62						
V 0085	Pyjama		£69.50						
V 0086	Nightshirt		£55						

☐ I WISH TO PAY BY CHEQUE PAYABLE TO DAVID NIEPER ☐ SWITCH ISSUE No. EXPIRY DATE ☐☐ ☐☐ MONTH YEAR TOTAL £ ☐

VISA ☐ CREDIT CARD NO. ☐☐☐☐ ☐☐☐☐ ☐☐☐☐ ☐☐☐☐

Signature: _____

Mrs/Miss/Ms/Mr: _____

Address: (CAPS PLEASE) _____

_____ Postcode: _____

Daytime Telephone Number: _____ OG03

Delivery within 7 days - max. 28 days. Full refund if returned within 14 days

David Nieper

ORDER NOW
FREE POSTAGE AND PACKING **01773 836000**
Saulgrove House Freepost Somercotes Derbyshire DE55 9BR

A forest for the nation

Phil Drabble sings the praises of a remarkable woodland initiative

Our 90 acre wood is surrounded by family-owned farms – some have herds of milking cows while others live by the plough or its modern juggernaut equivalent. They are all struggling forlornly against the most drastic rural change since the Industrial Revolution.

National media reports highlight the fact that to be a farmer, especially a dairy farmer, is more dangerous than to be a fireman. Far fetched as this may sound, it is true. The stress of working long hours combined with the constant threat of bankruptcy has led to many suicides among farmers. Let us hope that the government can come up with some practical help before the situation worsens.

Saved by bracken

Practical solutions can be found to many problems. Take the destruction caused to peat bogs by our desire for garden peat. Some bright spark has suggested that bracken – a nuisance in most places – could be cut and composted. Environmentalists think that this might reprieve precious peat bogs which Mother Nature has spent thousands of years creating.

Bracken is such a pernicious weed that it ruins vast areas of hill grazing for sheep and I hate it because it smothers wild flowers and young native hardwood saplings, including oaks, hornbeam and beech, for which our part of the ancient Forest of Needwood was once so famous.

National objective

Six years ago the National Forest Company was set up with the specific objective to create a multi-purpose forest covering over 200 square miles of the Midlands of England. That doesn't mean (of course) continous uninterrupted forest, but it does mean planting large areas dotted here and there. It makes my bit seem a bit puny – but I grasped at the straw in partnership with others.

The brains behind the scheme is Susan Bell, a woman of many talents. She trained as a journalist, qualified as a town-and-country planner and worked as an environmental consultant before being appointed by the Countryside Commission to lead the Development Team that drew up the strategy for the National Forest. The department of the Environment set up the National Forest Company in 1995, appointing her the chief executive.

The National Forest that Susan looks after is so immense that the Department of the Environment has improved the grant available to over

Susan Bell: architect of a forest for the future.

land – and owners do not agree to such schemes unless they are convinced it is for the good of all. Hedgerows have actually been planted, instead of being continually grubbed out.

A truly National Forest on such a scale has attracted the backing of an extraordinary range of big guns, from John Major to Tony Blair. They do not want – or cannot afford – to stand aside from this great project which, with luck, will still be with us at the end of the third millennium.

My friend Gerald Springthorpe wrote the definitive *Wildlife Rangers Hand Book*, which established him as an international authority on forests and what could be encouraged to survive in them. I remember he was worried that intruders would disturb wildlife in a wood within a mile of ours. A simple notice 'Please do not stand on the adders' did the trick. They took themselves off to other areas!

£3million for the year 2000. You can get a lot of trees for that, either by planting them or creating conditions that will allow them to spread naturally.

The 'Grow a Tree from Seed' campaign has won immense support and those who take the trouble to do some planting will not welcome strangers trampling on 'their' young trees, any more than I would welcome trespassers in my heronry scaring herons off their nests.

It is the sheer scale of Susan Bell's work that is so impressive. Over 80 per cent of the planting she has overseen during the past few years has been on privately owned

By the same token, if you make the area of a National Forest large enough, there can be room for all to enjoy it in harmony, though the fact takes time to sink in for some.

The New Year Honours included an OBE for Susan Bell – it was richly deserved. ∎